New and Improved Edition

How to Meet a Mensch* in New York

in New York

Robin Gorman Newman

❋ A decent, responsible person even your mother would love

New and Improved Edition

How to Meet a Mensch* in New York

Robin Gorman Newman

With Illustrations by Barbara McGregor

❀ *A decent, responsible person even your mother would love*

CITY & COMPANY
NEW YORK

ACKNOWLEDGMENTS

It has been my dream for as long as I can remember to write a book, and I would like to express my sincerest gratitude to all those who helped to make it a reality. Thanks to Susan Brady Konig for assisting in getting the project off the ground; Jack Scovil for his on-going belief in the book; Helene Silver for this exciting opportunity; Stacie Chaiken for her art direction; Barbara McGregor for her great illustrations; Lois Wyse for her creative input; and Kristin Frederickson for her day-to-day assistance.

A special thanks goes to my parents, Aaron and Sylvia, and sister, Barbara, for their unconditional love and support during my years in search of a Mensch; and to all my friends who played a role in this book, either by lending support and enthusiasm or by contributing insight and tips. — R.G.N.

Copyright © 1994, 1996 by Robin Gorman Newman
Illustrations Copyright © 1994 by Barbara McGregor

City & Company
22 West 23rd Street
New York, NY 10010

Printed in the United States of America

Design by Stacie Chaiken

Library of Congress Cataloguing-in-Publication Data
is available upon request.

First Edition 1994
Second Edition 1996

NOTE TO READERS: Neither City & Company nor the author has any interest, financial or personal, in the locations listed in this book. No fees were paid or services rendered in exchange for inclusion in these pages.

Information regarding addresses and phone numbers should always be verified, before setting out on your quest for the perfect mensch.

To the Mensch in my life—my husband—
without whose love, incredible support,
patience, and editing skills this book would
not have been possible.

◉ ◉ ◉

To my niece, Dorothy, who will one day
grow up and meet a Mensch of her own.

Table of Contents

❀ ❀ ❀

Introduction: Trust Me

⊚ ⊚ ⊚

Being single in the nineties and living in New York is an on-going challenge. If one of your goals is to meet an all-around nice guy even your mother would love, otherwise known as a Mensch, your work is cut out for you.

For the last ten years, I've been immersed in the so-called New York City meet/meat market, and I'm ready to tell all. So put yourself in my hands. I've done the Mensch scene, and I've won.

Trust me.

There is no right or wrong meeting strategy. Just accept the possibilities for meeting people in new and exciting ways; you might even learn something about yourself.

My suggestions range from singles travel to volunteer opportunities to sports activities to spiritual retreats. There are comments from both singles and couples based on their experiences, and I've noted Personal Picks—my special recommendations, indicated by a ✿—and included cost when I thought it would be a consideration.

Thanks to a Personal Pick, I met a Mensch four years ago who has since become my husband. It can happen to you—if you let it.

While I believe our meeting was Fate, you have to give Fate a nudge by putting yourself in situations that could expedite a fortuitous meeting.

Remember, just because you're both single doesn't mean you're a match. First you must identify those qualities that are critical to your happiness in a relationship. You might have to overlook his schleppy wardrobe and his unreasonable dislike of ethnic food. A guy may be a "Mensch-in-the-making," but if you are looking for Mr. Perfect, already packaged, better stay home with a good book.

While you may often feel as if you are game-playing, always remember that most of us really want the same thing: Ultimate Happiness. But, before we can be happy with someone else, we must be happy with our own lives.

So live life to the fullest. Start today. Don't put life on hold while you play the "Waiting vs. Dating Game." Single is not a synonym for quarantine. True love does not happen overnight, and it will not come via Fed Ex to your doorstep. Like the lottery, "You Must Be In It To Win It," and that means taking a risk or two.

Most of us are looking for ways to meet aside from the club and bar scene, so I have focused on other kinds of interesting and less obvious potential meeting methods. Some are exclusively for singles, and others invite all types, but offer singles appeal. Many seeking a quality relationship support nonprofit organizations either by volunteering their time or attending fundraising events. What more gratifying way to find the love of your life than through benevolence?!

In the hectic nineties, convenience is a key factor, and that is one reason why personal ads and chatting via online computer services are growing in popularity. Some people are taking active steps by throwing their own networking or "New Blood" parties, as one group of women calls it. Travel is an excellent way to meet new people, and so considerable space is devoted to this topic.

I hope this book will not only serve as a useful and informative guide, but also as a source of humor and inspiration. As you read it, keep in mind that across that volleyball net, at the airline ticket counter, or standing on the dance floor next to you may be just the person you've been searching for—and that person, that Mensch, has probably been waiting to meet you, too.

Trust me.

Know the Lingo: Menschspeak

You must know the lingo and speak the language, whether you're in pursuit or being pursued. While "Mensch" typically describes a "nice Jewish boy" (NJB), it is more commonly interpreted as a universal term synonymous with a person considered "prime marriage material" (PMM)—meaning a man easily characterized as warm, sincere, kind, down-to-earth, and bright, with "good earning potential" (GEP), and not GU ("geographically undesirable"). He is not only "good on paper" (GOP) because he meets your many criteria, but he's also someone you'd gladly take home to meet mom and dad—or better yet, mom's already booked the catering hall just based on a description of him.

The Elusive Mensch: A Quiz

A Mensch is certainly not easy to come by, but first one has to know one to find one. According to Webster's College Dictionary, a Mensch is a decent and responsible person. The American Heritage Dictionary defines the word as a person having admirable characteristics, such as fortitude and firmness of purpose. The following quiz is designed to help determine your personal Mensch Identifying Ratio (MIR).

If the guy has almost all qualities from column (A) and is limited to at most two from column (B), he rates high on the "Mensch scale."

Column A

FUNNY: more like Jerry Seinfeld than Jerry Lewis

— ◎ —

HONEST: shares bachelor party stories with you...but spares you details on the stripper

— ◎ —

ROMANTIC AND PRACTICAL: has a house account with 1-800/FLOWERS and dials it often

— ◎ —

AMBITIOUS: occasionally works weekends but is always home for dinner

Column B

CORNY SENSE OF HUMOR: does his Jackie Mason impression at every party

— ◎ —

TOO HONEST: shares bachelor party stories with you...he thought the stripper was "fine"

— ◎ —

PRACTICALLY BROKE: he spends hours on 1-900/HOT-MAMA trying to meet people

— ◎ —

WORKAHOLIC: takes his beeper to bed...but is not on call

Column A cont...   Column B cont...

WINES AND DINES: loves risotto con porcini and pronounces it perfectly

WHINES ABOUT DINING: if it's not on his discount card, you're not eating there

— ✺ —

INVESTMENT SAVVY: solvent, stable, and risk-free

NOT FINANCIALLY ASTUTE: thinks stock market means livestock

— ✺ —

EXERCISE ENTHUSIAST: lifetime member of New York Health and Racquet Club

EXERCISE ENTHUSIAST: swears by Richard Simmons

— ✺ —

FOOTBALL FIEND: Entices you to take in a game at the Meadowlands by taking you shopping in Secaucus

FOOTBALL FIEND: has Sports Phone programmed before his mother on speed dial

— ✺ —

NOT EXACTLY ON THE CUTTING EDGE OF FASHION: but looks great in his ten year old jeans

NOT EXACTLY ON THE CUTTING EDGE OF FASHION: doesn't know that flood pants were never in style

— ✺ —

SMART: interested in discussing the issues, not beating them to death

PSEUDO-INTELLECTUAL: reads the newspaper cover-to-cover and quizzes you over dinner

— ✺ —

SINCERE: says the sweetest things and puts it in writing, too

SAPPY: uses baby talk on the first date

— ✺ —

HANDY: took a course in the art of massage and does all his homework with you

TOUCHY-FEELY: has sweaty palms

Column A cont...   Column B cont...

CONVERSATIONAL: you can talk for hours and not get bored

CHATTY: talks in his sleep

— ❧ —

ATTRACTIVE: secure enough to shower all his attention on you

EGOTISTICAL: spends an hour in the shower and hogs the mirror

— ❧ —

LOVES TO TRAVEL: he's adventuresome...racked up frequent flyer miles on Fiji Air and Morocco Express

LOVES TO TRAVEL: frequents the Catskills

— ❧ —

BALDING: gracefully

BALDING: knows Sy Sperling personally

— ❧ —

HIS IDEA OF GREAT SEATS: a quiet table for two by the fireplace

HIS IDEA OF GREAT SEATS: nosebleed section... you can sneak down to the good seats at intermission

— ❧ —

GENEROUS: takes you to Saks on a birthday shopping spree

FRUGAL: doesn't pay more than $20 for a shirt and is proud of it

— ❧ —

LOVES TO COOK: Paul Prudhomme would be impressed

COOKING SKILLS: frozen chicken pot pies are his specialty

Alright, you know what to look for, Now where to look...

♥ 6 ♥

Mix 'n' Mingle

A Mensch is hard to identify at first glance, so when you go to a function sponsored by a singles organization, the key is to make conversation and be receptive, even if his dancing leaves a bit to be desired. Remember, it is not enough to simply place yourself in a meeting environment. You need to maintain a positive attitude and give off vibes that are inviting. Otherwise, no one will take the time to get to know you. If you go with friends, do not cling to them all night. Men know that women have a tendency to stay together, and this often inhibits the somewhat shy but desirable Mensch from making a move.

The party scene can be superficial and frustrating at times, but it is possible to meet someone. Try different groups to find the one that feels right for you in terms of the crowd it attracts. During the course of making the rounds, you may find that many of the same people frequent the functions of a particular group. While you may tire of seeing familiar faces, "it only takes one," as my mother has always said.

PERRY'S PARTIES
c/o The Roxy
515 West 18 Street
New York, NY 10011
Phone: 212/645-5156

Perry is king of the Friday night party catering to a Fire Island and Hampton's shareholders crowd. There is no admission charge if you arrive between 6:15 and 8:30 pm. To get on the mailing list, sign up at The Roxy.

Neil Siskind, 32, has attended Perry's Parties and reports, "Of all the singles parties, Perry's gets not only the largest crowd, but also the most diverse. The crowd is more upscale than many singles groups."

RICHNIK'S
362 West 23 Street
New York, NY 10011
Phone: 212/645-7755

Richnik's is one of NYC's supreme party-planning organizations and caters to the following age groups:

Parties with a Purpose
Parties for singles ages 22-35. Tavern on the Green is a popular site.

Perk's
Dances and after-work gatherings for singles ages 27-39.

Richnik's
Dances and after-work gatherings for singles ages 35+.

THE THIRTY-SOMETHING GROUP
P.O. Box 204
Lenox Hill Station
New York, NY 10021
Phone: 212/726-2424

Theme parties are held for singles ages 30-49 at clubs throughout NYC. (Note: Inquire about socials for singles in their 20s.)

DOC'S PARTIES
212-83 26 Avenue
Bayside, NY 11360
Phone: 718/279-8596

Personal Pick: Doc's offers parties for professional singles as follows:

Doc's
Parties in NYC for singles mostly in their 30s.

Doc's Plus
Parties in NYC for singles mostly in their 30s and 40s.

Synergy
Parties in NYC for singles mostly in their 20s.

The Diamond Club
Parties for singles ages 24-42 on Long Island at such places as Bruzells in Great Neck.

New Jersey Doc's
Parties for singles ages 24-42 at the Marriott in Teaneck, NJ.

METRO PROFESSIONAL & NU AGE SINGLES
P.O. Box 786
Forest Hills, NY 11375
Phone: 718/520-1267

Metro caters to singles ages 32-47, and Nu Age is for singles ages 38-54. Socials are held on Long Island and in Queens.

JEWISH SINGLES NETWORK GROUP
P.O. Box 220-204
Great Neck, NY 11022
Phone: 718/454-5277

Singles ages 22-39 attend parties at such places as Mai Tai.

HELAINE'S SENSATIONAL SINGLES
Phone: 516/624-7290

Helaine holds parties for business and professional singles every Thursday at various Nassau locations. Doors open at 8:00 pm, and a couple hundred singles ages 30+ dance, mingle, and enjoy the buffet.

MARION SMITH SINGLES
611 Prescott Place
North Woodmere, NY 11581
Phone: 516/791-4852 or 212/944-2112

Thanks to founder Marion Smith, singles ages 28-48 will not want for socializing opportunities. Parties are held at such NYC venues as Top of the Sixes, Tavern on the Green, and Atrium Club. The mailing list is close to 50,000 singles in the tristate area.

RIVERDALE SINGLES ASSOCIATION
P.O. Box 974
Pelham, NY 10803
Phone: 718/548-5598

Catering to singles ages 35+, there are dances, dinners, wine/cheese socials, and rap sessions held at various locations.

CALCULATED COUPLES
P.O. Box 335
Plainview, NY 11803
Phone: 516/932-4331

Singles ages 22-45 attend parties held on Sundays at 8:00 pm at various locations throughout Nassau. There is computer matchmaking and dancing.

NATIONAL ASSOCIATION FOR SINGLE ADULTS
P.O. Box 93
Plainview, NY 11803
Phone: 516/931-6523

This group has been offering events for ages 27-59 for nearly 20 years. To get on the mailing list, you must attend a function and sign up there.

LE JUDA AND SOPHISTICATES & QUEST
136 Garth Road, Suite 111
Scarsdale, NY 10583
Phone: 914/725-2551 (Le Juda) and 914/725-7540 (Quest)

Personal Pick: Le Juda serves Jewish singles ages 22-35, and Sophisticates is for singles 35-49, in NY, NJ, and CT. They send out monthly mailings listing singles dances held every weekend at various locations. Quest is for upscale professionals.

LORRAINE'S HIGH SOCIETY SINGLES
P.O. Box 211
Seaford, NY 11783
Phone: 516/795-6203

There are 3,000 members on a tristate mailing list, primarily upscale business/professional singles, ages 28-50. Weekly dances are held at various spots in Nassau, including the Roslyn Country Club.

LILY'S SINGLES NETWORK, INC.
Phone: 516/399-7689

Professionals in their 30s and 40s attend monthly parties, with discussions and dancing held at the Piping Rock in Westbury, Long Island. There are more than 250 people on the mailing list, and approximately 60 people attend each event. Buffet and hors d'oeuvres are served, and the atmosphere and crowd are upscale.

STACY'S PROFESSIONAL SINGLES
Phone: 516/997-4050

Every Wednesday night at Winners Circle in Westbury, singles ages 25+ gather and dance to music by a live D.J., and enjoy a complimentary buffet.

A GROUP OF JEWISH SINGLES
Deerfield Terrace and Academy Terrace
P.O. Box 390
Linden, NJ 07036
Phone: 908/925-3836 or 908/925-3845 (24-hour Hotline)

Co-sponsored by more than 40 congregations, A Group of Jewish Singles caters to three age groups: ages 20s & 30s, 35-49, and 49+. Activities include brunches, dessert receptions, trips, holiday parties, sports events, and coffeehouses. Locations throughout NJ vary.

SINGLE FACES
P.O. Box 211
Marlboro, NJ 07746
Phone: 908/462-2406 (Hotline)

There are 25,000 people on the mailing list. Approximately 400-500 singles ages 28-50 attend dances and events at various NJ locales.

Up, Up and Away

ꙮ   ꙮ   ꙮ

Sometimes it takes leaving New York to meet a Mensch from New York. In my eyes, travel offers the best of both worlds for singles. Since the objective of most trips is to see the sights, not just socialize, it's a great way to make new friends in a generally relaxed, risk-free atmosphere.

I speak from personal experience. Five summers ago, I needed a break from work, but original plans for a vacation fell through at the last minute. Since it was too late to recruit friends as travel companions, I searched for a tour that would present meeting opportunities. On a whim, I called the local Y in Flushing, Queens.

They advised me of a two-week trip offered by a group called Jewish Singles Vacations based in Massachusetts. The tour was to London and Paris, and while I had been to Paris as a college student, one can never see enough of this romantic city. Little did I know that Paris would take on a new, especially romantic meaning this time around. On this trip, I met the Mensch from Great Neck, Long Island, who became my husband.

Don't feel that you have to book a trip with a friend. The advantage of going on a singles tour is that you may request a roommate, and you are sure to befriend others in the group. While I do believe in Fate, you also have to help it along. Had I not gone to Europe alone, to this day I don't know if I would have met my husband.

CLUB MED
40 West 57 Street
New York, NY 10019
Phone: 800/CLUB-MED

Personal Pick: Club Med has more than 100 vacation villages world-wide and a cruise ship. "Hot" destinations for singles include Turkoise, Martinique, and Cancun. By day, you engage in sports, conversation, and sunbathing. Evenings consist of sumptuous dinners, a show, and dancing in the night club.

I went to Club Med in Guadeloupe, and while I had a great time, it attracts a primarily European crowd. So for all those who want to meet a dreamy Frenchman, give this club a try.

DOC'S TRAVEL
P.O. Box 20084
London Terrace
New York, NY 10011
Phone: 212/242-1402

While not expressly a travel organization, Doc's offers discounts on trips to Club Med, the Concord Resort Hotel, and other singles destinations.

RICHNIK'S
362 West 23 Street
New York, NY 10011
Phone: 212/645-7755

Personal Pick: Discounts are offered on Club Med, Hedonism, and cruise lines. Trips are for singles 22-60 to the Caribbean, Europe, Rio, Africa, Israel, etc. There are also weekends at resort hotels in upstate NY.

TRAVEL COMPANION EXCHANGE, INC. (TCE)
P.O. Box 833
Amityville, NY 11701
Phone: 516/454-0880

TCE is a nationwide match-up service for travel-minded singles. Members receive a newsletter listing members seeking compatible partners, travel companions, new friends, or travel-minded dates.

CAROLYN ROGERS TRAVEL
42 Remsen Street, Suite 4
Brooklyn, NY 11201
Phone: 718/875-3878

Carolyn's offers trips to Catskills hotels, Windjammer Barefoot
Cruises, Singleworld, etc.

MARION SMITH TRAVEL, INC.
611 Prescott Place
North Woodmere, NY 11581
Phone: 516/791-4852 or 800/698-TRIP

Personal Pick: Trips for singles in their late 20s-40s include tennis
vacations, skiing, whitewater rafting, cruises, Hedonism, Club Med,
and weekends at Club Getaway and various Catskill hotels.

UMBRELLA SINGLES
P.O. Box 157
Woodbourne, NY 12788
Phone: 914/434-6871 or 800/537-2797

This organization offers weekend trips to places like the Concord
Resort Hotel, Cape Cod, Quebec and both domestic and overseas
vacation packages. Singles tend to be on the 30+ side.

ULTIMATE TRAVEL
P.O. Box 679 Centuck Station
Yonkers, NY 10710
Phone: 212/978-8513 or 914/237-1913

Ultimate Travel recommends trips for singles and offers discounts on
Club Med, Club Getaway, Catskill hotels, ski packages, cruises, etc.

CONTIKI
1432 East Katella Avenue
Anaheim, CA 92805
Phone: 714/937-0611 or 800/466-0610

Contiki conducts trips attracting a predominantly singles crowd ages 18-35 only. Locales are exotic, and itineraries are adventurous.

David Freides, 33, who traveled with Contiki to Italy reports, "For people on a modest budget, Contiki offers affordable trips and opportunities to meet singles from around the world."

SOLO FLIGHTS
63 High Noon Road
Weston, CT 06883
Phone: 203/226-9993

There are trips for solo travelers and trips that are customized for singles groups. The moderately priced trips feature both domestic and overseas destinations. The tours attract a wide cross section of professionals ages 35+. Solo Flights also represents such companies as Club Med, Singleworld, and Windjammer Barefoot Cruises.

WINDJAMMER BAREFOOT CRUISES
1759 Bay Road, P.O. Box 120
Miami Beach, FL 33119-0120
Phone: 800/327-2601

Windjammer offers Singles Sailings to the Caribbean that attract all ages. The trips are ideal for the adventure-seeker who enjoys top-notch sailing in the company of an intimate few.

Meredith Gross, 34, went on a Windjammer Cruise and said, "It's a great way to relax. The activities vary depending on the island visited. The trip will be memorable, whether or not you meet the man/woman of your dreams."

CLUB EUROPA
802 West Oregon Street
Urbana, IL 61801
Phone: 217/344-5863 or 800/331-1882

Travel for ages 18-34 to Europe and Israel. Groups are usually 30-40 people, and trips are affordable.

SINGLE GETAWAYS
Wild Oats Tours, Inc.
356 Milburn Avenue
Millburn, NJ 07041
Phone: 800/376-6287

Single Getaways offers trips such as a week in Antigua and white-water rafting on the Colorado River. Groups range in size from 30-40 people, with a fairly even ratio of men to women, ages 26-42.

Expressly Jewish

AMERICAN JEWISH CONGRESS
International Travel
15 East 45 Street
New York, NY 10028
Phone: 212/328-0018

Personal Pick: Trips for both singles under 40 and 40+ are first rate. There are many worldwide destinations attracting professionals. Attend an orientation meeting before picking a trip.

92ND STREET Y
1395 Lexington Avenue
New York, NY 10128
Phone: 212/427-6000

The Y offers weekend getaways and trips throughout the US and overseas. While tours are not strictly for singles, Director of Tours and Travel, Batia Plotch, will gladly tell you how particular trips are sizing up.

SINGLE SCENES
P.O. Box 4172
Great Neck, NY 11023
Phone: 516/773-0922 or outside NY 800/767-7770

Jewish heritage and current lifestyles are a part of the overseas trips geared toward two groups of singles: ages 22-35 and ages 35-60.

JEWISH SINGLES VACATIONS
P.O. Box 211
Brookline, MA 02146
Phone: 617/782-3396

Personal Pick: This is the group that worked for me! They offer affordable trips throughout the US and Europe and attract an intimate, congenial group of professionals ages 22-45, principally from New York.

PREMIER JEWISH SINGLES
9378 Olive Street, Suite 120
St. Louis, MO 03132
Phone: 800/444-9250

Premier offers vacation packages for singles in their mid 20s-early 50s. Destinations range from Israel to Istanbul to New Zealand. Lists of travelers are mailed out prior to trips so people can meet.

The following Jewish organizations sponsor trips to Israel designed as fundraisers/consciousness-raising experiences:

AMERICAN FRIENDS OF THE ISRAEL MUSEUM
Associates Division & Young Patrons Group
Phone: 212/683-5190

AMERICAN SOCIETY FOR TECHNION
Israel Institute of Technology
Phone: 212/262-6200

JEWISH NATIONAL FUND
Future Leadership Division
Phone: 212/751-4848

STATE OF ISRAEL BONDS
New York New Leadership
Phone: 212/644-2663

UJA-FEDERATION
Missions Department
Phone: 212/818-9100 ext. 352

Specialized Groups

COUNTRY CYCLING TOURS
140 West 83 Street
New York, NY 10024
Phone: 212/874-5151

This bike club offers bicycling and walking tours in upstate NY, VT, and winter jaunts to the Caribbean. There are one-day excursions and longer trips attracting active singles in their 30s.

GALLIVANTING
The Club For Adventure
515 East 79 Street, Suite 20F
New York, NY 10021
Phone: 212/988-0617 or outside NY 800/933-9699

Gallivanting caters to athletic, professional singles ages 25-55. The worldwide tours feature hiking, safaris, rafting, cycling, hot air ballooning, etc., along with fine dining, dancing, history, and culture.

OUTDOOR BOUND
18 Stuyvesant Oval, Suite 1A
New York, NY 10009
Phone: 212/505-1200

This group offers trips to upstate NY, VT, PA, ME, etc. It attracts primarily singles in their 20s-40s who enjoy hiking, canoeing, rafting, kayaking, and camping.

OUTDOOR SINGLES
P.O. Box 656674
Fresh Meadows, NY 11365
Phone: 718/353-5506

Trips feature hiking, canoeing, beach picnics, swimming in mountain lakes, rafting the rapids, mountain horseback riding, bicycling, skiing, etc. Members are generally professionals ages 25-50.

SINGLES FOR SAILING
SINGLES FOR SKIING
Box 1043
Manhasset, NY 11030
Phone: 718/279-2680

This organization offers both day and weekend sailing and affordable ski weekends and trips for people in their late 20s-60.

WILDERNESS TRIPS WITH CHARLIE COOK
P.O. Box 655
Pomona, NY 10970
Phone: 914/354-3717

Personal Pick: Trips attract predominantly singles in their 20s-40s. Trips feature hiking, camping, and backpacking.

Weekend Getaways

CLUB GETAWAY
P.O. Box 606 Lenox Hill Station
New York, NY 10021
Phone: 212/935-0222

Personal Pick: This Club Med-style resort in Kent, CT attracts singles mostly in their 20s-40s. Sports-oriented, it features cabin accommodations, casual dress, good food, and lively nightlife. Look for special theme weekends.

Deena Nussbaum, 32, went to Club Getaway and is now married to Robert Heller, 33. "I felt funny going alone, but Bobby and I met at night under the stars by the volleyball court. As we strolled back to my cabin, little did I know that this was the prelude to our walk down the aisle."

THE CONCORD RESORT HOTEL
Kiamesha Lake, NY 12751
Phone: 800/727-7388

The Concord sponsors singles weekends for more than 100 singles ages 21+. Activities include champagne parties, dancing, volleyball, and the dating game. The hotel is huge, and meeting opportunities are endless.

WEEKENDS UNLIMITED
136 Garth Road, Suite 111
Scarsdale, NY 10583
Phone: 914/725-1225 or 800/388-8850

Affiliated with the Jewish singles group Le Juda, Weekends Unlimited offers weekends for Jewish singles age 20+ to resort hotels like the Concord and the Pines in the Catskills. Holiday weekends are particularly popular.

NEW JERSEY YM-YWHA CAMPS
21 Plymouth Street
Fairfield, NJ 07006
Phone: 201/575-3333

Jewish singles ages 20s-40s stay at the Camping Center, Milford, PA. The mood is casual, and people are down-to-earth. Accommodations are rustic.

POCONO WHITEWATER ADVENTURES
Route 903
Jim Thorpe, PA 18229
Phone: 717/325-3655

Day trips and weekend getaways feature rafting down the Lehigh River, mountain biking trips, canoeing, etc. No experience required —just a desire for adventure and socializing. Singles primarily in their 20s and 30s.

Summer Shares

DEERWOOD
236 East 75 Street, Apt. 4A
New York, NY 10021
Phone: 212/288-7370 or 800/676-3337

Personal Pick: If you like a rustic social setting, Deerwood is the place for you. Located in Great Barrington, MA, this summer share community attracts professional singles in their late 20s-early 40s. Activities include tennis, swimming, softball, horseback riding, sailing, volleyball, dancing, a movie theater, a game room, and nearby Tanglewood.

FIRE ISLAND & THE HAMPTONS

If the beach is your thing, you might want to consider a summer share in a house on either Fire Island or the Hamptons. No cars are permitted on Fire Island, and the dress is informal. The bar scene is where it's at in the evening, unless you "party hop" from one house to the next. Quoque is a popular Hamptons area. Dance clubs and bars are the primary social opportunity in the evening. Check out the *Village Voice* classified ads, where houses are listed starting in February. You can arrange to visit the person running the house who will show you photos and discuss potential housemates. You may enjoy meeting people through the interview process, even if you ultimately decide not to take a share. *New York* magazine and Doc's Newsletter (see page 10) also advertise summer share houses. Richnik's (page 9) throws Summer Share Parties at clubs in NYC where you meet representatives from these houses.

For the Sports-Minded

◎ ◎ ◎

*I*f sneakers, hiking boots, or bike shorts are your dress code of choice, there are many opportunities to meet other like-minded singles with a penchant for sports. Granted, few of us would probably qualify for the Olympics, but it doesn't take the athletic ability of a pro to participate in sporting activities that might be conducive to meeting a Mensch.

Whether it be tennis, golf, volleyball, skiing, biking, rafting, skating, hiking, rock climbing, or even scuba diving, it's the effort that counts rather than the skill level. Of course, a certain proficiency tends to enhance the experience, but it is possible to meet people through group lessons or just giving it your best. Enthusiasm is contagious. So what if your team loses or capsizes the raft; it's all in the spirit of fun and adventure, and a Mensch would certainly be a good sport.

With some of these activities, like joining a league or frequenting a tennis club, the more regular a participant you become, the greater your chances of seeing familiar faces and getting to know people. Many find it easier to ask someone for a tennis date than a typical Saturday night on the town. Meeting through sports helps break down barriers of communication...not to mention the fact that you already share an interest. You can then progress to attending sporting events together, and Saturday night at your favorite neighborhood bistro may only be a field goal away (especially if they have ESPN).

Outdoor Oriented

MOSAIC OUTDOOR MOUNTAIN CLUB
OF GREATER NEW YORK
P.O. Box 998, Midtown Station
New York, NY 10018
Phone: 212/696-8666

Personal Pick: While not expressly for singles, many eligible professionals in their 30s and 40s participate in hiking, ski trips, bike trips, and ice skating. There are more than 200 members.

NEW YORK-NEW JERSEY TRAIL CONFERENCE
232 Madison Avenue
New York, NY 10016
Phone: 212/685-9699

Personal Pick: This is a nonprofit federation of more than 80 hiking clubs and over 9,000 individuals working to build and maintain trails and promote conservation. A list of clubs and activities is featured in Trail Walker, the official newspaper of NY-NJ Trail Conference.

Peter Reiser, 31, who has participated in many hikes, reports: "People are generally friendly and talkative on hikes because you are together for an entire day, and it is a relaxed environment. People also tend to be more open when they're out of the city."

OUTDOOR SINGLES
P.O. Box 656674
Fresh Meadows, NY 11365
Phone: 718/353-5506

Personal Pick: This is an outdoor adventure and social club for single professionals ages 25-50. Activities include hiking, rollerblading, comedy nights, canoeing, beach days, picnics, tubing, biking, rafting, swimming, horseback riding, and skiing.

HIGH ANGLE ADVENTURES, INC.
5 River Road
New Paltz, NY 12561
Phone: 914/658-9811 or 800/777-CLIMB

High Angle Adventures offers rock climbing instruction at all levels. The school is 90 minutes from NYC. Many singles in their 20s and 30s attend.

MOUNTAIN SPORTS
1738 Highway 31
Clinton, NJ 08809
Phone: 908/735-6244

Mountain Sports Adventure School offers rock and ice climbing instruction. They also teach mountain bike riding. Climbing gear, tents, backpack, and camping accessories are provided. Participants include many singles, primarily in their 20s and 30s; 80% are men.

APPALACHIAN MOUNTAIN CLUB
5 Joy Street
Boston, MA 02108
Phone: 617/523-0636

Members are hikers, backpackers, conservationists, kayakers, canoeists, photographers, skiers, birdwatchers, bicyclists, and campers—all people who love the outdoors. There are chapters for NY-Northern Jersey and CT.

Leagues

THE NEW YORK URBAN PROFESSIONALS
ATHLETIC LEAGUE
200 West 72 Street, Suite 68
New York, NY 10023
Phone: 212/877-3614

New York Urban Professionals compete in a coed volleyball league held at various gyms throughout NYC. Most players are college grads or professionals in their 20s and 30s. Matches are held weekly, and there are 200+ teams.

TRACS OF NEW YORK
A Division of Yorkville Sports Assoc.
1123 Broadway, Suite 306
New York, NY 10010
Phone: 212/645-6488

Personal Pick: TRACS organizes sports leagues for coed touch football, softball, basketball, and volleyball. A newsletter offers information on sports activities and health and fitness.

EASTERN TENNIS ASSOCIATION
USTA LEAGUE
Phone: 718/381-2366

Many singles in their 20s and 30s join this tennis league and play mixed doubles matches at locations throughout NYC. You must get rated so you will be matched with players of your skill level.

WESTCHESTER CORPORATE LEAGUE
Phone: 914/968-0611

Both individuals and corporations participate in this coed volleyball league attracting many singles in their 20s-early 40s. The season lasts 10 weeks, and there are novice, intermediate, and advanced divisions.

Tennis Parties

CROSSTOWN TENNIS
14 West 31 Street
New York, NY 10001
Phone: 212/947-5780

Fridays at 8:00 pm. Intermediate and above players. Up to 30 people attend a night.

MANHATTAN PLAZA RACQUET CLUB
450 West 43 Street
New York, NY 10036
Phone: 212/594-0554

Friday and Saturday nights at 9:00 pm. Intermediate and above players. Between 18 and 24 people attend per night.

MIDTOWN TENNIS
341 Eighth Avenue
New York, NY 10001
Phone: 212/989-8572

Friday nights at 9:00 pm. Not advisable for basic beginners. Average of 40 people attend a night.

RICHNIK'S
362 West 23 Street
New York, NY 10011
Phone: 212/645-7755

Held at Roosevelt Island Racquet Club on Friday and Saturday nights at 8:00 pm. All levels welcome. Between 40 to 70 people attend a night.

SUTTON EAST TENNIS
488 East 60 Street
New York, NY 10022
Phone: 212/751-3452

Friday and Saturday nights at 9:00 pm. All levels above beginner. About 30 people attend a night.

MARION SMITH SINGLES
611 Prescott Place
North Woodmere, NY 11581
Phone: 516/791-4852 or 212/944-2112

Personal Pick: Tennis parties are held at East River Tennis Club in Long Island City, Jericho/Westbury Tennis Club and Rockville Racquet Tennis Club on Long Island, and Sound Shore Indoor Tennis Club in Westchester. Players are all levels in their late 20s-40s. Inquire about special Tennis Socials, Mixed Doubles Tournaments, and trips to Amherst Adult Tennis Camp.

SUE'S SINGLES
Phone: 516/935-1586

Tennis parties are held two evenings a month at Syosset Tennis Academy. Each session attracts approximately 60 to 100 singles ages 30-60.

Tennis Camps

TOTAL TENNIS
Box 1106 Wall Street Station
New York, NY 10268
Phone: 718/636-6141

This adult tennis camp is located in the Pioneer Valley at the Wiliston-Northampton School in Easthampton, MA. Enrollment is limited to 60 players on all levels. There is a welcome barbeque, movies are shown, and trips to local discos and night spots are arranged.

AMHERST TENNIS CAMP
Box 2271
Amherst College
Amherst, MA 01002
Phone: 413/542-8100 or 800/526-6388

Personal Pick: Amherst Tennis Camp offers clinics for singles. Players are put through a rigorous tennis program of drills and matches, and in the evening there are planned social activities. Instruction is available for all levels of play, and you can stay for a week or a weekend.

Biking

NEW YORK CYCLE CLUB
P.O. Box 199 Cooper Station
New York, NY 10276
Phone: 212/886-4545

Rides are led by volunteers to various NY and NJ destinations. Monthly meetings are held in NYC.

FIVE BOROUGH BICYCLE CLUB
American Youth Hostels, Inc.
891 Amsterdam Avenue, Room 128
New York, NY 10025
Phone: 212/932-2300 ext. 243

This is the meeting place of three affiliated clubs: the Five Borough Bicycle Club, Ski Club, and Hike Club. The Bicycle Club programs include day and weekend bicycle trips, continuing education, and special events.

Volleyball

EDUCATIONAL ALLIANCE EMANU-EL MIDTOWN Y
344 East 14 Street
New York, NY 10003
Phone: 212/674-7200

Coed volleyball is held every Wednesday from 8:30-10:30 pm. Attracts singles ages 20-40.

FLUSHING JEWISH COMMUNITY COUNCIL
41-60 Kissena Boulevard
Flushing, NY 11355
Phone: 718/460-5069

Competitive volleyball matches are held on Tuesdays at 7:30 pm at the Garden Jewish Center in Flushing. Mostly men in their 20s and 30s attend. Bowlers meet on the third Saturday of each month at Sterling Lanes in New Hyde Park. Between 40 to 50 singles attend, primarily in their 30s and 40s.

CENTRAL QUEENS YM & YWHA
The New Jewish Professionals Group
67-09 108 Street
Forest Hills, NY 11375
Phone: 718/268-5011

Volleyball games are held every Sunday at 7:15 pm and attract singles mostly in their early 30s.

MID-ISLAND JEWISH COMMUNITY CENTER
45 Manetto Hill Road
Plainview, NY 11803
Phone: 516/822-3535

Personal Pick: Volleyball games are held for singles on Wednesdays from 7:00-10:00 pm. Approximately 35 people ages 18-32 attend, with a typically even male/female ratio.

Nathan Malkiel, 33, who was a regular until meeting his wife, Regina, said, "Everyone I know who went there got married. In fact, since I met my wife at volleyball, I also proposed to her there. For women, it's particularly good because the ratio works in their favor."

Golf

THE ROLAND STAFFORD GOLF SCHOOL
P.O. Box 81
Arkville, NY 12406
Phone: 914/586-3187 or 800/447-8894

The school has several US locations, but the one nearest to NYC is Windham in the Catskills. On a given weekend, between 55 to 65 people ages 25-45+ take group instruction and mingle at mealtime. The atmosphere is comfortable and casual, and many singles attend.

Miscellaneous

MANHATTAN PLAZA HEALTH CLUB
482 West 43 Street
New York, NY 10036
Phone: 212/563-7001

If rock climbing has always intrigued you, now's your chance to give it a shot. You will learn the basic skills and put them to the test on the climbing wall at this health club. You don't need to be a member.

NEW YORK ROAD SKATERS ASSOCIATION
328 East 94 Street
New York, NY 10128
Phone: 212/534-7858

This is the largest club in the country, with over 1000 active members who participate in rollerblading. Activities are recreational, competitive, educational, and instructional. Leisure skates are held in Central Park.

PAN AQUA
101 West 75 Street
New York, NY 10023
Phone: 212/496-2267

Pan Aqua offers scuba training that attracts professionals in their mid 20s-late 30s. Approximately 50-60% of students are single.

SOUND SAILING CLUB
P.O. Box 1307
Ansonia Station
New York, NY 10023

This is the largest nonprofit organization in the tristate area for singles interested in sailing. To receive information, write to them at the above address. Instruction is offered, in addition to sails and cocktail parties in NYC and Greenwich, CT.

Parties for a Purpose

＠ ＠ ＠

Nonprofit is the way to go in the nineties because involvement with these organizations offers gratification in more ways than one. By investing your time, energy, and money as a volunteer and/or fundraising partygoer, you may experience a fruitful social life and feel good about making a contribution to a worthwhile cause.

In addition to attending social functions, you can join a committee of professionals who meet during the year as volunteers to plan benefits. The more involved you choose to be, the better you will get to know others who share your sensibility and desire to "do good." This is certainly an appealing trait...and one that you would hope to find in a Mensch. If a person shows concern for others, it's a good bet that he will treat you well.

While socializing is not the focus of most organizations listed, it can be the icing on the cake. Many organizations offer volunteer opportunities, but require a serious commitment in terms of your time and skills. You might want to take this into consideration when selecting an organization to support.

When perusing this chapter, please keep in mind that it is by no means comprehensive. If there is a particular cause you feel strongly about, you should give them a call. Most organizations can never have enough volunteers.

CANCER CARE, INC.
1180 Avenue of the Americas
New York, NY 10036
Phone: 212/302-2400

Cancer Care is a nonprofit social service agency that helps cancer patients, their families, and friends cope with the impact of cancer. The Junior Committee, mid 20s-late 30s, plans three annual fundraisers attracting roughly 500 people.

CROHN'S & COLITIS FOUNDATION OF AMERICA, INC. (CCFA)
386 Park Avenue South, 14th Floor
New York, NY 10016
Phone: 212/679-1570

The Business & Professional Division is a volunteer group of young professionals dedicated to aiding in the search for a cure for Crohn's disease and ulcerative colitis. They plan three events a year that attract singles in their early 20s-late 40s. A big party is the annual Mardi Gras Casino Carnival. There are also volunteer opportunities.

CYSTIC FIBROSIS FOUNDATION
60 East 42 Street, Room 1563
New York, NY 10165
Phone: 212/986-8783

This nonprofit health organization is dedicated to finding a cure for Cystic Fibrosis. The Junior Committee plans two black tie events a year catering predominantly to singles ages 23-38. Monthly meetings are held and other events are run.

FRESH AIR FUND
1040 Avenue of the Americas
New York, NY 10018
Phone: 212/221-0900

This not-for-profit agency provides free summer vacations to disadvantaged NYC children. The Benefit Committee attracts eligibles and marrieds ages 25-40 who attend benefits held at the Armory and Tavern on the Green. Volunteer opportunities exist behind the scenes at parties and during the year by participating in calling nights, camp visits, etc.

LEUKEMIA SOCIETY OF AMERICA
600 Third Avenue, 4th Floor
New York, NY 10016
Phone: 212/697-7848

Personal Pick: Society Ties is the young volunteer group dedicated to planning events and raising money for research to find the cause and cure for leukemia and its related diseases. Professionals, mostly singles in their 20s and 30s, meet monthly to organize two annual fundraisers, plus smaller events. Parties have included a comedy night, a casino night, and a spring gala.

NATIONAL MULTIPLE SCLEROSIS SOCIETY
30 West 26 Street
New York, NY 10010
Phone: 212/463-2094

Personal Pick: The Manhattan Society is a volunteer group of professionals, ages 20-45, committed to the fight against multiple sclerosis (MS). Meetings are the first Monday of every month where members socialize, plan events, and speakers discuss issues pertinent to the fight against MS. A popular party is held on the Intrepid.

NEW YORK BENEVOLENCE COUNCIL, INC. (NYBC)
P.O. Box 882 Ansonia Station
New York, NY 10023
Phone: 212/969-0955

NYBC is a nonprofit organization with volunteers dedicated to serving the NYC community. It sponsors and organizes charitable events for social and human service organizations. There are volunteer opportunities and three fundraisers a year attracting professionals in their 20s and 30s.

NEW YORK CARES
116 East 16 Street
New York, NY 10003
Phone: 212/228-5000

Personal Pick: New York Cares oversees volunteer projects including feeding the hungry, rehabilitating housing for the poor, visiting homebound seniors, collecting coats for the homeless, assisting people with AIDS, etc. To get involved, you attend an orientation meeting and volunteer either with specific organizations, or work behind-the-scenes on planning comedy nights, wine tastings, and the winter gala. A monthly calendar lists projects.

UNITED CEREBRAL PALSY OF NEW YORK CITY, INC.
105 Madison Avenue
New York, NY 10016
Phone: 212/683-6700

United Cerebral Palsy of New York City is the sole voluntary health agency devoted to the problems and needs of children and adults with cerebral palsy and related disabilities. The NY Contemporary League plans benefit parties, held twice a year, that attract professionals in their 20s and 30s. Venues have included Au Bar, China Club, and Broadway Grill.

KIPS BAY BOYS & GIRLS CLUB
1930 Randall Avenue
Bronx, NY 10473
Phone: 718/893-8600

Kips Bay works to enhance the quality of life for boys and girls in NYC, with an emphasis on the special needs of the economically, socially, and recreationally deprived. The Junior Committee, ages 25-35, holds an annual spring ball, and Christmas and summer parties.

SINGLES FOR CHARITIES, INC. (SFC)
P.O. Box 302
East Norwich, NY 11732
Phone: 516/338-9252

SFC provides volunteer services to nonprofit organizations on Long Island. A monthly newsletter lists volunteer opportunities with such groups as the Long Island Philharmonic, the Association for the Help of Retarded Children, and the Long Island March of Dimes. Activities for members include weekend trips, singles rap and dances, and meet and mingle nights.

Jewish Organizations

ALYN-AMERICAN SOCIETY FOR HANDICAPPED CHILDREN IN ISRAEL
19 West 44 Street, Suite 1418
New York, NY 10036
Phone: 212/869-8085

Alyn is Israel's only orthopedic hospital and rehabilitation center for physically handicapped children. The Society is dedicated to the care and treatment of children suffering from crippling diseases or trauma after accidents. The Young Leadership Division attracts many single professionals ages 25-42. Benefit parties, attended by approximately 800, are held at such places as the Water Club and Club USA.

AMERICAN COMMITTEE FOR THE WEIZMANN INSTITUTE OF SCIENCE
51 Madison Avenue
New York, NY 10010
Phone: 212/779-2500

The Weizmann Institute of Science is a world-renowned center of scientific research and graduate studies in Israel. The Weizmann League is comprised of young professionals dedicated to promoting and supporting the Institute. The annual major fundraiser brings together more than 300 supporters, including singles ages 21-45. Events are held at galleries and museums. Parlor meetings feature scientists who report on their research.

AMERICAN FRIENDS OF TEL AVIV UNIVERSITY
360 Lexington Avenue
New York, NY 10017
Phone: 212/687-5651

Tel Aviv University in Israel is a major center of teaching and research offering an extensive range of study programs in the arts and sciences. The Young Professionals Division plans events that include wine tastings and other cultural/educational social activities. It attracts professional singles in their mid 20s-40s.

AMERICAN ISRAEL PUBLIC AFFAIRS COMMITTEE (AIPAC)
3 East 54 Street, 9th Floor
New York, NY 10022
Phone: 212/750-4110

This organization lobbies Congress and the Administration on legislation affecting Israel. Young Leadership educates and promotes pro-Israel political involvement among professionals in their 20s and 30s. They host political and educational lectures and fundraising events, including annual Policy Conferences in Washington. Those particularly committed may join the Manhattan Club for Singles for a $250 a year contribution.

AMERICAN SOCIETY FOR TECHNION (ATS)
Israel Institute of Technology
810 Seventh Avenue
New York, NY 10019
Phone: 212/262-6200

The Technion is Israel's only comprehensive technological and scientific university and its largest applied research center. The mission of ATS is to convince the leadership of the American Jewish community that the future of a secure and economically independent Israel is in high technology, and that the future of high technology in Israel is at the Technion. The NYC Chapter sponsors lectures attracting an intellectual group in their 30s and 40s.

ANTI-DEFAMATION LEAGUE (ADL)
823 United Nations Plaza, Suite 900-VA
New York, NY 10017
Phone: 212/490-2525

The ADL is one of the nation's oldest and largest civil rights/human relations organizations. The Young Leadership Division sponsors three major benefits a year that attract singles in their 20s and 30s. They have run such fundraisers as the Inaugural Presidential Ball at the UN.

DOROT, INC.
262 West 91 Street
New York, NY 10024
Phone: 212/769-2850

Dorot is dedicated to improving the lives of frail, homebound, and homeless elderly in NYC. Volunteers are involved with holiday package deliveries and friendly visits. Dorot Associates encourage awareness of Dorot and support its programs among professionals in their early 20s-mid 40s. Theater benefits, comedy nights, and wine and food tastings are examples of events sponsored by the Associates, comprised of both singles and marrieds.

FRIENDS OF AKIM USA, INC.
Association for the Rehabilitation
of the Mentally Handicapped in Israel
327 Lexington Avenue
New York, NY 10016
Phone: 212/684-1942

AKIM is a voluntary organization dedicated to improving the lives of the mentally handicapped in Israel. The Young Professionals Division plans events attracting singles in their 20s and 30s, including a Friday Night Dinner Series, art shows, cocktail receptions, and auctions.

HADASSAH
The Women's Zionist Organization of America, Inc.
250 West 57 Street, Suite 1801
New York, NY 10107
Phone: 212/765-7050

Personal Pick: Hadassah is the largest and one of the oldest American Zionist/Jewish Women's Organizations with service rooted in Jewish education and carried out through programs in America and Israel in medicine, education, career training, and development. Vanguard brings together Jewish singles ages 25-40 to participate in cultural and social events. These have included a trip to Atlantic City, ice skating, a country western dance, apple picking, a wine and cheese party, and white water rafting. They also have branches in Nassau (Phone: 516/766-2725) and Suffolk (Phone: 516/499-3999).

Janet Baer, 27, and Mark Becker, 32, met through their involvement with Suffolk Vanguard and said, "Vanguard is the greatest place to get to know Jewish people in a non-pressure social environment. We both joined to meet people and make new friends, and little did we know that we'd meet our future mates."

JERUSALEM FOUNDATION
60 East 42 Street, Suite 1936
New York, NY 10165
Phone: 212/697-4188

The Jerusalem Foundation raises funds for the development of the city. The New Leadership Group works to build a following of young people, many single, in their late 20s-40s who get involved, feel a commitment, and visit Jerusalem. The Group meets at various NYC locations for evenings with diverse speakers. There are approximately 60 active members, and fundraisers have been held at such places as The Coffee Shop and Carnegie Hall.

JEWISH GUILD FOR THE BLIND
15 West 65 Street
New York, NY 10023
Phone: 212/769-6239

The Guild is a non-sectarian, not-for-profit health care agency serving blind and visually impaired New Yorkers. The Associates Division is a volunteer committee of professionals, both singles and married ages 21-45 who raise funds to support The Guild's programs and services. They work on committees involved with fundraising and planning events, including a cocktail party at Tavern on the Green and a gala at The Harmonie Club.

JEWISH NATIONAL FUND (JNF)
964 Third Avenue, 6th Floor
New York, NY 10155
Phone: 212/751-4848

JNF raises funds for planting and maintaining forests throughout Israel, building roads, parks, and outdoor recreational and tourist facilities, developing irrigation systems, dams and reservoirs, etc. The Future Leadership Division holds parties at such places as The Baja and The Water Club that attract single professionals ages 25-40. They also sponsor lectures throughout the year.

SIMON WIESENTHAL CENTER
342 Madison Avenue
New York, NY 10173
Phone: 212/370-0320

Parties for a Purpose

The Simon Wiesenthal Center is an international center for Holocaust remembrance, the defense of human rights, and the Jewish people. The Leadership Board for the Society plans activities including parlor meetings held at private homes and receptions at the Jewish Museum. Singles and marrieds in their 20s-40s attend.

STATE OF ISRAEL BONDS
575 Lexington Avenue, Suite 600
New York, NY 10022
Phone: 212/644-2663

Personal Pick: This organization offers securities issued by the government of Israel for the development of Israel's economy. New Leadership events include parlor meetings, gallery and museum exhibitions, cocktail parties, and receptions for Israeli government officials and American business leaders. A highlight is the NY New Leadership Sabra Society dinner. In addition to the admission charge for each social event, a purchase of a State of Israel Bond is required. A sophisticated group of people, including many singles, ages 25-40, attend.

Melissa Hubsher, 33, served on the NY New Leadership Executive Board and had this to say, "Every year I've been involved with Israel Bonds, people have met and married through their involvement with the organization."

UJA-FEDERATION
130 East 59 Street
New York, NY 10022
Phone: 212/836-1499 (Hotline)

Personal Pick: The Leadership Development Divison of UJA-Federation is dedicated to increasing the awareness among young professionals of the needs of Jewish people in NY, Israel, and worldwide. There are countless opportunities for both singles and marrieds ages 22-40 to meet and mingle. These include fundraising events, community service projects, educational lectures, social receptions, leadership training, and travel. There are specialized groups to meet others in a particular profession including Entertainment, Marketing, Communications, Sales, Real Estate, and Banking and Finance. For those ages 35-55, there is Business Professionals of NY who meet for philanthropic, cultural, and social purposes.

Cultural Encounters

@ @ @

New York offers vast opportunities to meet through cultural activities. Theater enthusiasts, music lovers, dance devotees, museum-goers, and art afficionados can each find an outlet for their interest.

Okay, so you like Pavorotti, and he likes The Grateful Dead; you studied ballet since age five, and he has two left feet; you like Renoir, and he likes Norman Rockwell. Don't give up hope. Tastes can be cultivated, and abilities developed, if both parties are willing.

As a theater enthusiast, I could not have married someone who did not share this interest, even if his level of interest did not extend to The Ridiculous Theatre Company. (He now likes their work.)

When it comes to theater, you may choose to attend a benefit for a theater company, see a play with other singles, or if the footlights draw you to center stage, take an improvisational acting class or audition for a community theater. When improvising, all inhibitions are stripped, and there is certainly little need for an opening liner; you've passed the stage of needing an ice breaker. Laughter inevitably wins out in the end...and everyone wants a Mensch with a sense of humor.

Theater

CHICAGO CITY LIMITS
1101 First Avenue
New York, NY 10021
Phone: 212/888-5233

Chicago City Limits offers a complete training program in improvisational theater, and has a current enrollment of more than 100 students. Classes meet once a week for 2 1/2 hours. If you'd like to sit in on a class, call ahead and come prepared to participate. This is a fun way to meet new people in a small class setting that promotes conversation through performance.

CUCARACHA THEATRE
500 Greenwich Street, Suite 302
New York, NY 10013
Phone: 212/966-8596

If soap operas are to your liking, you might want to venture over to Cucaracha Theatre where they present Underground Soap, an Obie-winning serial comedy performed every Friday at 10:00 pm. Set in a loft-like space, there is mingling after the show around the bar often frequented by singles ages 25-40. The crowd varies, and the theater commonly attracts a downtown type.

MANHATTAN CLASS COMPANY
120 West 28 Street
New York, NY 10001
Phone: 212/727-7722

Two to three fundraising events are held during the year. These range from parties at Manhattan clubs to a soap opera bowl-a-thon, where you get to meet some of your favorite daytime stars. The crowd is mixed ages, both singles and couples.

ROUNDABOUT THEATRE
1530 Broadway
New York, NY 10036
Phone: 212/719-9393

The Dewar's Singles Series attracts single theater-goers in their 30s and 40s. A total of four plays are offered per season, and one night of each run is designated for singles. After the show, there is mingling at a cocktail party in the lobby. Open bar and food are included in the ticket price. The theater accommodates 500 people, and it is advisable to sign up early since this is a popular series.

SECOND STAGE THEATRE
P.O. Box 1807
2162 Broadway
Ansonia Station, NY 10023
Phone: 212/787-8302

Personal Pick: Offering four plays a year, a Singles Night is held for each show of the season. Subscribers have the opportunity to mingle at pre-performance receptions in the lobby. Approximately 100 singles attend.

YOUNG PLAYWRIGHTS, INC.
321 West 44 Street, Suite 906
New York, NY 10036
Phone: 212/307-1140

An annual benefit features an engaging panel discussion of playwrights, along with a cocktail party. It attracts a congenial group of supporters for the work of Young Playwrights, and it tends to be a sell-out. The age range is mixed, both singles and couples.

Music

CHAMBER MUSIC SOCIETY OF LINCOLN CENTER
70 Lincoln Center Plaza
New York, NY 10023
Phone: 212/875-5788

Three out of the twelve concerts held each year are designated for the Chamber Music Club, part of The Chamber Music Society of Lincoln Center. Geared toward New Yorkers in their 20s and 30s, the special series of three Friday night concerts is each preceded by a reception at 6:45 pm.

FESTIVAL CHAMBER MUSIC SOCIETY
750 Third Avenue, Suite 2400
New York, NY 10017
Phone: 212/678-6970

The Young Professionals Group attracts professionals in their 20s and 30s who attend concerts at Merkin Concert Hall. There is a pre-concert dinner buffet and a champagne reception after the concert. Approximately 70 people, mostly single, attend. The male/female ratio is fairly even. Five concerts are held in NYC and three are held in Westchester.

Julia Hicks, 29, a member of the board for two years says, "The good thing about the Society is that with a planned social event before and after the concerts, it gives you a focus. It attracts people open to experimenting with various cultural forms, which can lead to interesting conversation because it's novel for many young professionals."

NEW YORK PINEWOODS FOLK MUSIC CLUB
31 West 95 Street
New York, NY 10025
Phone: 212/316-3780 or 212/666-9605

The Folk Music Society of New York, also known as the Pinewoods Folk Music Club, is a not-for-profit organization founded to further the enjoyment of folk music in the NYC area through concerts, singing parties, and weekends of folk music in the country. There are approximately 800 members ages 20+.

NEW ORCHESTRA OF WESTCHESTER
111 North Central Avenue, Suite 425
Hartsdale, NY 10530
Phone: 914/682-3707

Singles in their mid 30s-60s attend the Symphony Singles Concert Series which includes a party after each performance.

CLASSICAL MUSIC LOVERS' EXCHANGE (CMLE)
P.O. Box 31
Pelham, NY 10803
Phone: 800/233-CMLS

CMLE brings together single music lovers for the purpose of sharing musical interests. Members fill out biographical profiles and receive a monthly newsletter featuring bios on other members. You may request copies of the lengthier bios of those of particular interest. Communication is then initiated via mail or phone. There are more than 1,000 members, mostly professionals in their mid 20s-50s.

Dance

COUNTRY DANCE NEW YORK, INC.
P.O. Box 878, Village Station
New York, NY 10014
Phone: 212/459-4080

Country Dance New York is a volunteer organization of people dedicated to the enjoyment and study of English and American traditional dance, music, and song. Dances are held weekly at various NYC locations. There are 500 members of all ages, predominantly singles.

DANCE MANHATTAN
119 East 15 Street, 4th Floor
New York, NY 10003
Phone: 212/228-0844

Dance Manhattan offers seven classes a week in West Coast Swing dancing, attracting many singles ages 20s-40s. A group class is a good way to learn, and socials are held with both taped and live Big Band music. They also teach ballroom dancing, Latin/hustle, country western, etc. Check out the Rhythm & Blues/Swing Dance attracting 200 people at The Continental Club.

FRED ASTAIRE DANCE STUDIOS
666 Broadway, 2nd Floor
New York, NY 10012
Phone: 212/475-7776

The tango, waltz, fox trot, cha-cha, merengue, rumba, and salsa are just some of the dances you can learn, either in private lessons or in a group. Socials are held monthly on Thursdays and Saturdays, in addition to regional events. Many singles ages 30-50 attend. (If this Village location is not convenient, check your phone book for others. There are some in Queens and Nassau, too.)

NEW YORK SWING DANCE SOCIETY
P.O. Box 1512
New York, NY 10009
Phone: 212/NY-NYSDS (696-9737)

The New York Swing Dance Society is a not-for-profit arts organization dedicated to the revival and promotion of Swing dancing to live Big Band music. The Society sponsors Savoy Sunday dances at 7:00 pm at The Continental Club. There are approximately 800 members, including many singles in their 30s and 40s.

STEPPING OUT
1780 Broadway, 4th Floor
New York, NY 10019
Phone: 212/245-5200

This dance instruction studio offers private and group instruction and holds dances that attract many singles in their 20s-60s.

NEW YORK METROPOLITAN COUNTRY MUSIC ASSOCIATION INC.
P.O. Box 201
Bellrose, NY 11426
Phone: 718/763-4328

Country western dances are held every Saturday night in Glendale. Free dance lessons are given from 8:30-9:00 pm, and the dance goes until 1:00 am. Members receive a bimonthly newsletter and flyers announcing activities. Dances are attended by 150 people, both couples and singles age 18+.

Museums

AMERICAN FRIENDS OF THE ISRAEL MUSEUM
10 East 40 Street, Suite 1208
New York, NY 10016
Phone: 212/683-5190

Brought together by an interest in art and a commitment to Israel and the Israel Museum, Associates and Young Patrons sponsor educational, art-oriented, and social activities in conjunction with curators, gallery owners, and collectors. The Associates Division has approximately 70 members in their 20s and early 30s, primarily singles. They hold an annual spring fundraiser/dance, and socializing with an educational/artistic orientation is encouraged via visits to galleries and private collections. The Young Patrons Group, for those in their late 30s-50s, attracts more marrieds than singles. There are approximately 55 members.

AMERICAN MUSEUM OF NATURAL HISTORY
Central Park West at 79 Street
New York, NY 10024
Phone: 212/769-5166

Membership in the Junior Council goes to support Museum activities. You receive exclusive invitations to events attended by singles and marrieds in their 20s and 30s. These include the Annual Winter dance at the Museum, exhibit previews, private screenings, and discussions with some of the world's leading scientists and research teams. There are typically three events a year.

JEWISH MUSEUM
1123 Fifth Avenue, Suite 509
New York, NY 10010
Phone: 212/675-9474

Members of New Generation receive general museum benefits, in addition to invitations to events exclusively for individuals and couples under 40. These include dinner socials, cocktail parties, tours, and the annual Masked Ball in Celebration of Purim held in March at the Waldorf-Astoria. There are also opportunities for participation on committees.

METROPOLITAN MUSEUM OF ART
1000 Fifth Avenue
New York, NY 10028
Phone: 212/570-3948

The Junior Committee holds a benefit dance for the Museum in the spring, and a cocktail party in the fall. The average age of attendees is 27. Membership in the Committee is by nomination only.

MUSEUM OF MODERN ART
11 West 53 Street
New York, NY 10019
Phone: 212/708-9514

The Junior Associates is an affiliate group of the Museum of Modern Art who participate in and support programs concerned with modern and contemporary art. The group, ages 20-35, attends Museum activities and events scheduled outside the Museum. This includes visits to private collections, private curatorial tours of exhibitions at the Museum and film screenings. The Junior Associates are also invited to all of the Museum's black-tie events.

NEW MUSEUM OF CONTEMPORARY ART
583 Broadway
New York, NY 10012
Phone: 212/219-1222

The New Group is a committee of young people who contribute to the growth of the Museum by supporting the work of young artists. They sponsor educational programs and events including a spring benefit dance and gallery exhibitions. Mostly singles in their late 20s-30s attend.

WHITNEY MUSEUM OF AMERICAN ART
945 Madison Avenue
New York, NY 10021
Phone: 212/570-3697

The Lobby Gallery Associates is a group of 100 young professionals interested in being involved with educational and social activities at the Whitney and supporting the Museum's operations. Many benefits are held throughout the year open to members and the general public.

Miscellaneous

ARTISTS SPACE
38 Greene Street, 3rd Floor
New York, NY 10013
Phone: 212/226-3970

Artists Space is a not-for-profit contemporary cultural center committed to providing opportunities, professional assistance, and financial support to artists. Activities include a film and video series, art exhibitions, panel discussions and an annual spring benefit.

ARTS & BUSINESS COUNCIL, INC.
Business Volunteers for the Arts (BVA)
25 West 45 Street, Room 707
New York, NY 10036
Phone: 212/819-9277

Personal Pick: BVA recruits volunteers to assist arts organizations in NYC by offering services ranging from accounting to legal counsel to public relations. There are approximately 200 members, many of whom are single in their late 20s-40s. Volunteers meet at workshops, cocktail receptions, and behind the scenes tours of local arts organizations. There is a committee of volunteers who plan events, many of which serve as fundraisers for the Arts & Business Council.

GEN ART
240 Mercer Street, Suite 1206
New York, NY 10012
Phone: 212/473-6898

Gen Art seeks undiscovered artists in NY and introduces them to young collectors, enabling them to support themselves through the exhibition and sale of their work. Exhibitions are held throughout the year. A newsletter and calendar of upcoming events includes seminars, lectures, etc.

92ND STREET Y
1395 Lexington Avenue
New York, NY 10128
Phone: 212/996-1100

Designed for singles in their 20s-40s, the Y has numerous classes called Singles Minded, including offerings for those with cultural interests: Museums: A New Perspective; Jazz Finders; Music: A Brief Introduction; Dance! Dance! Dance!; and Comedy Tonight.

Computer Compatibility

*T*he city never sleeps, and if you're a night owl, this is the socializing method for you. It is accessible 24 hours a day, come rain, shine, sleet, or snow, in the convenience of your home. Cabin fever may take on a new meaning if true love heats up over the computer lines. While it would be quite costly to buy a computer expressly for the purpose of boosting one's social life, an added benefit for existing computer-owners is the opportunity to engage in discussions with others of similar interests.

For those of you who have been contemplating the purchase, let this be further incentive in the value of the investment.

Think of it this way—the up side is you don't have to leave the comfort of your home for the chance to chat with new people. You don't have to get decked out, recruit a friend, or pick a destination. The down side—okay, you don't know what the person looks like, but if you are fortunate enough to "connect" with someone who you ultimately meet, and if it's a match made in "information highway heaven," you can sell one of your PCs and actually come out ahead of the game.

By the way, intelligence is one trait you would expect to find in a Mensch, and at the very least, you know he knows how to use a computer.

EAST COAST HANG OUT (ECHO)
179 Franklin Street
New York, NY 10013
Phone: 212/292-0900

ECHO offers more than 40 conferences on culture, love, NY, sex, etc. There are approximately 1,500 members, mostly New Yorkers in their 30s and 40s, both singles and marrieds. The first Monday of every month, ECHO members gather at Art Bar in Greenwich Village at 8:00 pm. It's a good way for face-to-face encounters when you tire of the computer screen.

PANIX
15 West 18 Street
New York, NY 10011
Phone: 212/877-4854

Panix has approximately 3,500 members, mostly in NYC and the tristate area. Popular News Groups for mingling are Events and People. They also sponsor social events.

AMERICA ONLINE
8619 Westwood Center Drive
Suite 200
Vienna, VA 22182
Phone: 703/448-8700 or 800/827-6364

There are approximately 700,000 members, and popular "Rooms" for meeting include Virtual Bar, LaPub, Romance Connection, and The Flirt Nook. Major departments include lifestyles and interests like Travel, Shopping, Computing and Software, and People Connection, where people chat about a multitude of subjects.

PRODIGY
445 Hamilton Avenue
White Plains, NY 10601
Phone: 800/PRODIGY

With more than two million members nationwide, Prodigy is
America's most popular interactive network. Approximately 250,000
singles nationwide over the age of 18 are on-line. There are more
than 800 public bulletin board topics ranging from travel to Jerry
Seinfeld. There is also a Personals section browsed by 80,000 people
a month. The ratio of men to women is eight to one. You can connect to the Prodigy service through a regular telephone line
attached to a home computer with a modem.

*Robin Paul, 23, and John White, 30, met through Prodigy when they both
went on-line to chat with other singles. They tapped into a group of Long
Islanders ages 17-35, and after three months of exchanging messages, they
decided to meet. They're now a couple. Robin said, "When you get home
from work, it's often too late to go out with friends, but with Prodigy, you
don't have that problem. You can get to know someone without the pressures
of a date. At the very least, you know you have computers in common, and
if it doesn't work out, you can go back to being friends."*

WHOLE EARTH 'LECTRONIC LINK (WELL)
1750 Bridgeway, Suite A200
Sausalito, CA 94965
Phone: 415/332-4335

The Well is part of the Internet, a worldwide system connecting
thousands of computers. You connect to The Well with your own
computer and take part in discussions with other people. You can
also exchange messages with individuals worldwide in their early
20s-mid 50s. The Well is divided into more than 200 discussion areas
called conferences, and each consists of different topics including
Singles; Social Responsiblity & Politics; Body, Mind, Health;
Recreation; and Generation X (for those born in the sixties).

COMPUSERVE
5000 Arlington Centre Boulevard
Box 20212
Columbus, OH 43220
Phone: 800/848-8199

CompuServe is an international network that gives you access to nearly 2,000 on-line products and over one million users. CB Simulator is where people of all ages participate in on-line discussions, ranging from the serious to frivolous. There are hundreds of conversational forums including Sailing, Health & Fitness, and Working from Home.

The Personal Approach

♪ Matchmaker ♪
♪ Matchmaker

⊚ ⊚ ⊚

Personal ads and dating services may not be for everyone, but many a Mensch has found love through these methods.

You may answer or place an ad in a mainstream publication, singles publication, or newsletter distributed by a singles organization. Whatever outlet you select, give consideration to the type of reader it attracts. For example, if an intellectual sort is not your dream partner, the New York Review of Books may not be for you.

While reading personal ads, you may feel like you need a translator to decipher the acronyms. No one speaks in acronyms, but suddenly here you have little else to go by. If you can't relate to this language, have a friend write an ad for you. It is hard to be objective when writing about yourself, and it's interesting to see yourself through someone else's eyes.

A matchmaker may also help you see yourself by identifying strengths, weaknesses, and how you may be perceived by others. Remember, however, that no two dating services are alike. For this reason, you might want to call several to request information. Don't hesitate to ask questions, and do not feel obligated. You should not be pressured into making a decision. This is not a method for the frugal, but it can ultimately be cost effective by allowing you to maximize the time you spend on actual dates, as opposed to attending socials or writing and responding to personals.

The Personal Approach

Personals—Publications

JEWISH SENTINEL
21 West 39 Street, 2nd Floor
New York, NY 10018
Phone: 800/783-1131 ext. 34 (to place ad)
or 900/976-3450 ext. 34 (to hear ads)

Call 24 hours a day, seven days a week to place a free print ad in
"The Jewish Meeting Place" that runs in this free NYC weekly
newspaper.

JEWISH SINGLES NEWS
P.O. Box 1053
New York, NY 10028
Phone: 212/348-1755 (to place ad) or 900/988-4897 (to hear ads)

There is no cost to place an ad in "Jewish Dialogue" that runs in this
monthly newspaper. (There is a comprehensive listing of singles
events and the newspaper sponsors parties for different age groups
two or three times a year at such places as The Roxy and the
Barbizon Hotel.)

JEWISH WEEK
1501 Broadway
New York, NY 10036
Phone: 212/921-0643

If a mate of like mind and spirit is what you seek, this is the newspaper for you.

LEARNING ANNEX
116 East 85 Street
New York, NY 10028
Phone: 212/935-5077 (to place ad)
or 900/880-3000 (to hear ads)

Ads may be placed free of charge in the "Learning Annex
Personals" section by sending in the coupon in the magazine.

NEW YORK MAGAZINE
2 Park Avenue
New York, NY 10016
Phone: 212/779-7500

Personal Pick: This is the publication of choice for city-wise singles. Though "Strictly Personals" ads are on the pricey side, you may meet your knight in shining armor on a "white gold" horse.

NEW YORK POST
1211 Avenue of the Americas
New York, NY 10036
Phone: 800/457-3142

If you want to meet a sports fanatic, this is the publication for you. There is no charge to place a "Post Personal." Ads run every Monday, Wednesday, and Friday for up to two weeks.

Debbie Chin, 36, opted to place a "Post Personals" ad after having observed many a man on the Long Island Railroad reading the sports section. "It's exciting because you never know if the person behind the voice could be Mr. Right. Initially, it's a bit intimidating because it feels like a blind date, but the difference is that you choose who you want to meet."

NEW YORK REVIEW OF BOOKS
250 West 57 Street, Room 1321
New York, NY 10107
Phone: 212/757-8070

Published every two weeks, this newspaper is sold primarily in book stores. Readers are highly educated professionals and there is a higher male than female readership, mostly ages 40+.

NEWSDAY
2 Park Avenue
New York, NY 10016
Phone: 800/248-3283 (to place ad)
and 900/880-1199 (to hear ads)

There is no charge to place an ad in "Introduction," the personals section. This is the paper to reach Long Island suburbanites.

The Personal Approach

**VILLAGE VOICE PERSON-TO-PERSON
CLASSIFIEDS**
36 Cooper Square
New York, NY 10003
Phone: 212/475-5555 (to place ad)
and 900/800-MORE (to hear ads)

The *Village Voice* publishes a free weekly "Person To Person" supplement available in freestanding boxes on street corners throughout NYC. There is no charge to write and record a "Voice Mail Response Line Ad," which runs for three weeks.

SINGLE TIMES
P.O. Box 1015
Valley Stream, NY 11582
Phone: 516/565-9100

There is no cost to run an ad in "Personal Touch By Phone" published in this monthly newspaper with a circulation of 55,000 throughout NY, NJ, and CT.

SPOTLIGHT MAGAZINE
126 Library Lane
Mamaroneck, NY 10543
Phone: 914/381-4813

When you place an ad in "The Singles Source" in this monthly magazine, you get both a personalized mailbox for written reponses and a personalized voice mailbox. Messages and letters can be retrieved for four weeks .

GANNETT SUBURBAN NEWSPAPERS
1150 Wehrle Drive
Williamsville, NY 14221
Phone: 800/466-6832

Personal Pick: There is no cost to place an ad in "Personal Connections," which will run for three weeks throughout Westchester County.

DATE BOOK
257 Ely Avenue
Norwalk, CT 06854
Phone: 203/866-6617 (to place ad)
and 900/226-1060 (to hear/respond to ads)

This free monthly publication provides a comprehensive listing of events read by over 50,000 active singles in Westchester, Fairfield, and New Haven counties.

SINGLES ALMANAC
725 Route 440
Jersey City, NJ 07304
Phone: 800/ADSINGLE (to place ad)
and 900/476-1310 (to hear ads)

If you want to reach the masses, opt for this monthly newspaper, which targets a readership of more than 30,000 tristate area singles in their late 20s-mid-50s. When you subscribe to Singles Almanac, you get a free personal ad. (Singles Almanac has a Hotline, 1-900-446-EVENT, that readers can call to hear about events.)

NEW JERSEY MONTHLY
P.O. Box 920
Morristown, NJ 07963
Phone: 201/539-8230 or 800/669-1002

If you live in NJ, this might be the publication for you.

Personals—Organizations

OUTDOOR SINGLES
P.O. Box 656674
Fresh Meadows, NY 11365
Phone: 718/353-5506

All adventure-oriented recipients of the newsletter published by Outdoor Singles can send in a free personal ad.

MARION SMITH SINGLES
611 Prescott Place
North Woodmere, NY 11581
Phone: 516/791-4852 (to place ad)
& 900/772-7740 (to hear/respond to ads)

Ads in "The Right Connection" run in Marion Smith's bimonthly newsletter and a quarterly mailer sent to nearly 50,000 singles in the tristate area. In addition, ads are displayed at weekly parties sponsored by the organization.

NATURAL CONNECTIONS
P.O. Box D-900
Pomona, NY 10970
Phone: 914/354-2499 or 800/474-3100

Natural Connections is a network of active people interested in nature and the outdoors. Members range in age from their early 20s-70s. When you join, you write a "Personal Profile" about yourself which is distributed to other members. In turn, you receive the Profiles of current members. New listings are sent every two months.

LE JUDA & SOPHISTICATES
136 Garth Road, Suite 111
Scarsdale, NY 10583
Phone: 914/725-2040

Personal Pick: More than 25,000 Jewish singles ages 20-49 receive this monthly "Personal Touch" column.

Matchmaking/Dating Services

CLASS
116 Central Park South, 8B
New York, NY 10019
Phone: 212/613-9191

Class serves singles ages 20-50+. Call to make an appointment, at which time you will be given all the details, including rates, which are said to be "reasonable."

CROSSROADS
321 East 43 Street
New York, NY 10017
Phone: 212/972-3594

There are large, theme-oriented events where personal introductions are made; small "by invitation only" parties where a high degree of compatibility is assured; and activities may include skiing, tennis, concerts, etc. In addition, there is a personalized referral service for members who prefer one-on-one meetings. The majority of members are college-educated with above average levels of cultural and social awareness and ages range from 19-70.

GODMOTHERS, LTD.
25 Central Park West
New York, NY 10023
Phone: 212/245-7175

Founded by Abby Hirsch, Godmothers is a romance counseling service for the professional/executive men and women. While Hirsch and her staff get to know their clients personally to suggest matches, the primary means of meeting is the quarterly newsletter, "Highly Classified: A Preview." You write a brief description of yourself that runs in the newsletter mailed to the 600 or so members. From the listings, you choose those members you would like to meet.

INTRODUCTIONS CLUB, INC.
170 West End Avenue, 8N
New York, NY 10023
Phone: 212/877-0723

The Personal Approach

The Club is for successful Jewish professionals ages 30-55. After a one-on-one interview, psychoanalyst Dr. Barbara Chasen will let you know if she can assist you. Members are introduced to other singles and parties are held on occasion.

PEOPLE LINK
337 West 70 Street
New York, NY 10023
Phone: 212/769-0551 or 800/272-LINK

There are more than 400 members in their 20s-70s. When you join, you write a profile of yourself and you review books of bios to choose those of interest. People Link also sponsors members-only boat rides, comedy nights, trips, whitewater rafting, and buffet socials.

JEWISH DATING SERVICE
1260 New Britain Avenue, Suite 203
West Hartford, CT 06110
Phone: 203/561-3250

You fill out a 100-question application and go through an interview with a representative to determine the kind of person suitable for you. The age range is 20-70, and you are guaranteed at least 12 matches. There are thousands of members. Price quotes are not given over the phone.

THE RIGHT STUFF
An Introduction Network
P.O. Box 873
Upper Montclair, NJ 07043
Phone: 800/988-5288

The Right Stuff offers graduates and faculty of Ivy League, Seven Sisters, and other top schools the opportunity to meet members of the opposite sex ages 20-72. To join, you provide a short profile and a complete bio. You then receive a monthly mailing of profiles provided by all members of the opposite sex. You can request bios of those of interest, along with photos, and you may contact that person by mail or phone.

Wining and Dining

*A*s the saying goes, the way to a man's heart is through his stomach...even if you're not the one doing the cooking. Dinner groups, cooking classes, wine tastings, and lunchtime dating are all great meeting methods.

Food has been known to play an active role in romance. My sister tells a funny story of her first meeting with her now husband who dropped popcorn kernels on her lap during a baseball game. (You had to be there.)

Okay, so you may not be able to outdo Julia Child or even your potential mother-in-law in the kitchen, but a Mensch would appreciate the effort and maybe even be able to whip up something himself. Of course, it wouldn't hurt if he brought a bottle of Beaujolais Nouveau, which you both acquired a penchant for in the wine-tasting class where you met. This scenario sure beats take-out seven nights a week, even if you are on a first name basis with the Domino's delivery boy.

AMERICAN INSTITUTE OF WINE & FOOD
c/o Freundlich Associates
333 East 30 Street, Apt. 5K
New York, NY 10016
Phone: 212/447-0456

The American Institute of Wine & Food promotes a broad exchange of information and ideas among consumers and professionals. The NY area chapter offers wine and beer tastings that attract singles and marrieds in their 30s and 40s. There are also special festivals and ethnic neighborhood tours, seminars, educational programs, etc.

INTERNATIONAL WINE CENTER
231 West 29 Street, Suite 210
New York, NY 10001
Phone: 212/268-7517

The Center offers wine programs ranging from classes to stand-up tastings to members-only seated wine-tastings for the International Wine Club. The average age is 35.

IT'S JUST LUNCH
120 East 56 Street, Suite 730
New York, NY 10022
Phone: 212/644-0022

Personal Pick: It's Just Lunch is an easy and fun way to meet new people over a casual lunch date. When you join, you complete an application and go through a one-hour interview. The service is not computer-based, but has a hands-on personal approach. After a compatible partner is selected, you are called and told all about the match. It's Just Lunch coordinates the time and place of meeting, and you just show up. There are more than 300 members, all professionals ages 23-60.

LEARNING ANNEX
116 East 85 Street
New York, NY 10028
Phone: 212/570-6500

Personal Pick: **Wine Tasting with Willie Gluckstern**
This class will help you understand the fundamentals of wine appreciation. At least 20 wines or champagnes are tasted at each session. There are also a host of other classes such as Beer Tasting, a Social Evening at The Comic Strip (with pizza), Progressive Dinner Parties, and a Fine Chocolate Tasting.

THE NATURAL GOURMET
INSTITUTE FOR FOOD AND HEALTH
48 West 21 Street, 2nd Floor
New York, NY 10010
Phone: 212/645-5170

The Institute offers a weekly Friday Night Dinner made with fresh market produce and organic grains and beans. Food is served buffet style and 30-50 people converse in a friendly, casual atmosphere. The age range is mixed and the number of singles vary on a given night. Reservations are necessary. They also offer over 30 classes ranging from cooking techniques to healing cuisines.

NEW SCHOOL FOR SOCIAL RESEARCH
60 West 12 Street
New York, NY 10011
Phone: 212/229-5690 or 800/544-1979

Wining and Dining

Cooking for Singles: Great Meals in Minutes for One or Two
Learn how to prepare simple, yet elegant meals in less than one
hour. The cost is $180, with a materials fee of $55. A meal with wine
is served at each session, limited to 14 people. (Note: The New
School also offers a wide range of wine-tasting classes.)

92ND STREET Y
1395 Lexington Avenue
New York, NY 10128
Phone: 212/996-1100

Wine: The Art of Buying and Tasting
This is one of the Y's classes for "Singles Minded," ages 20-45. The
cost is $100 for six sessions.

THE SINGLE GOURMET
133 East 58 Street
New York, NY 10022
Phone: 212/980-8788

The Single Gourmet, the International Social Dining Club, brings
people together to share good food and drink while engaging in
conversation in pleasant surroundings. Several dinners are offered
monthly at all types of restaurants in NYC and NJ. A newsletter
advises members of upcoming events, and reservations are required.
When you join, you fill out an application that includes age, and
you will be seated with people close to your age group at dinners.
(The Single Gourmet also plans special events such as private
screenings, tennis matches, horse shows, sporting events, and trips.)

HARRIET LEMBECK
WINE & SPIRITS PROGRAMS
54 Continental Avenue
Forest Hills, NY 11375
Phone: 718/263-3134

These programs instruct professionals and connoisseurs who want
to experience the pleasures of wines and spirits. Director Harriet
Lembeck, and various guest speakers, offer lively, full-participation
tastings held at the NY Helmsley Hotel. The ten-week wine program, in particular, attracts people ages 21-40.

SINGLES BON VIVANT (SBV)
P.O. Box 1405
Summit, NJ 07902
Phone: 908/273-6868

Singles Bon Vivant is an association of single men and women who gather socially for relaxed evenings, conversation, and excellent cuisine at fine restaurants in northern NJ. Members are in their mid 20s-senior citizens. A monthly newsletter is sent to members, detailing dining opportunities and other information. There are six to eight dinners a month, and sometimes a champagne brunch on Sunday. Reservations are required. (SBV also offers trips to places such as Lake George and the Caribbean.)

CONVERSATIONS BY CANDLELIGHT
One Huyler Avenue
Tenafly, NJ 07706
Phone: 201/567-2082 or 201/567-6308

Conversations by Candlelight brings together professional singles of all ages for gourmet dinners at the home of founder Joan Braner. Approximately 24-32 people attend, with an even ratio of men to women. Parties are by invitation only. (If reading books or seeing movie classics and discussing them with others appeals to you, inquire about Joan's other groups—Great Books and Classic Movies.)

Better Yourself

@ @ @

City life can be a grind. That's when a retreat or a little self-pampering can work wonders for your health and maybe even your social life. After all, a Mensch should be of sound mind and body.

If you feel good about yourself, it shows, and you are that much more attractive to others. You might even meet your soul mate in an atmosphere of spirituality and wellness—at a spa, holistic retreat, workshop, or new age expo. Unlike the often pretentious social scene of many NYC gyms, a spa offers a more low-key environment with countless meeting opportunities—even your masseuse could turn out to be the man of your dreams. Or perhaps, strategically placing your aerobics step next to a muscle-bound Jack LaLanne look alike, could lead to an amorous workout for two.

Getting in touch with yourself can also improve your chances of connecting with someone else. Classes pertaining to spirituality, healing and renewal may work wonders. You might discover that you and a fellow student have the same karma, or maybe you were even together in a previous life.

JEWISH MEDITATION CIRCLE
West Side Institutional Synagogue
122 West 76 Street
New York, NY 10024
Phone: 212/799-1335

Singles and marrieds of all ages and denominations attend meditation classes.

LEARNING ANNEX
116 East 85 Street
New York, NY 10028
Phone: 212/570-6500

The Learning Annex offers courses taught by experts in their fields, often high-profile authors and lecturers. You can call up to be put on their mailing list to receive a publication listing classes or you can get a copy in freestanding boxes on street corners throughout NYC. Consider classes given by M. Scott Peck, M.D., the author of *The Road Less Traveled*, addressing life, love, spirituality, and personal growth; Dick and Tara Sutphen who teach "Reincarnation: Find the Cause of Your Karma," and Ariela and Shya Kane who conduct "Free Your Mind, Free Your Life."

NEWLIFE EXPO
218 West 72 Street, Suite 2FE
New York, NY 10023
Phone: 212/787-1600

Billed as The Symposium for Health, Environment & Spirit, this Expo is held twice a year in NY and other US cities. There are more than 200 exhibits, and approximately 20,000 people attend the three-day event. There is music, bodywork sessions, psychic readings, lectures and workshops on holistic health, alternative medicine, etc.

92ND STREET Y
1395 Lexington Avenue
New York, NY 10128
Phone: 212/996-1100

The Center for Adult Life & Learning at the 92nd Street Y conducts personal growth seminars, workshops, and classes promoting greater self-awareness and personal development. These include "Writing

Your Spiritual Autobiography," "Meditation: An Individual Journey," and "Changing Your Life...Right Now."

TOWN HALL
123 West 43 Street
New York, NY 10036
Phone: 212/840-2824

"A Course in Miracles," led by renowned author and lecturer Marianne Williamson, is offered monthly at 7:30 pm. Approximately 1,500 people with an interest in spiritualism and self-help attend.

BODY, MIND & SOUL
191 Walt Whitman Road
Huntington Station, NY 11746
Phone: 516/423-8300

Body, Mind & Soul offers a comprehensive holistic approach to better health and spiritual awareness. This retailer sells natural vitamins, new age books, and unique gifts, and hosts workshops on subjects ranging from Advanced Taoist Meditation to Music Therapy. There is also a Singles Networking Group, conducted by the Center for Self Empowerment, Inc. Another offering is Singles' Success Strategies, billed as "a must for singles seeking permanent relationships or simply improving the quality of their lives." Sign the mailing list when you visit the store to receive a monthly Calendar of Events. You might also call the CENTER FOR SELF EMPOWERMENT, INC. (516/921-2325) to inquire about other Singles Networking activities held at different locations.

NEW AGE HEALTH SPA
Neversink, NY 12765
Phone: 914/985-7600 or 800/682-4348

In the Catskill Mountains, New Age offers exercise programs, rap sessions, lectures, and a wide variety of personal services, including meditation treatment. The spa attracts singles and married professionals, mostly in their 30s and 40s, and tends to have a larger ratio of women to men. Meeting opportunities exist over meals in the dining room, at lectures, and just through general participation. The spa accommodates up to 70 guests.

Spa Lovers Take Note: To find a spa, fitness resort, or holistic retreat, call Spa Finders at 212/475-1000.

OMEGA INSTITUTE
FOR HOLISTIC STUDIES
260 Lake Drive
Rhinebeck, NY 12572
Phone: 914/266-4444 or 800/944-1001

Omega Institute is a holistic education center at the forefront of personal and professional development in subjects ranging from health and psychology to multicultural arts and spirituality. More than 10,000 participants attend workshops and conferences each year on its campus in Rhinebeck, NY. Trips are also arranged. Inquire about the Workshop for Singles who want to learn the secret to a lasting relationship. Offered periodically, it attracts eligibles predominantly in their 30s and 40s.

NEW CENTER FOR HOLISTIC HEALTH
EDUCATION & RESEARCH
6801 Jericho Turnpike
Syosset, NY 11791-4413
Phone: 516/364-0808

The New Center offers training in acupuncture, massage, and a wide array of counseling. Classes in Yoga and Tai Chi attract singles in their early 20s+.

ELAT CHAYYIM
THE WOODSTOCK CENTER FOR HEALING AND RENEWAL
P.O. Box 127
Woodstock, NY 12498
Phone: 914/679-2638 or 800/398-2630

Elat Chayyim is a retreat center where people experience a contemporary Jewish spiritual path that integrates the body, emotions, and intellect. Courses include such offerings as Sex, Passion and God, Holistic Strategies for Stress Management, Health and Well-Being, and Beginners Yoga Intensive. There are also tennis courts, a pool, volleyball courts and an indoor jacuzzi. Attendees are marrieds and singles mostly in their 30s and 40s.

CANYON RANCH IN THE BERKSHIRES
Bellefontaine, Kemble Street
Lenox, MA 01240
Phone: 800/742-9000

Personal Pick: Canyon Ranch offers the ultimate health and fitness experience...whether your goal is weight loss, destressing, fitness, pampering, or general wellness. There is typically an even ratio of men to women, and the crowd is mixed. Singles tend to be in their mid 30s-45. Meeting opportunities exist through mingling in classes, meals, evening lectures, etc.

Meeting on Common Ground

๑ ๑ ๑

ttending singles events at a synagogue or Jewish community center is not limited to the deeply religious. Many Jewish singles have a desire to marry within the religion, and the venues cited in this chapter can serve as a "Mensch mating ground." Some synagogues offer religious instruction, but these classes are not addressed in this book. The focus here is on social activities designed to bring people of like mind and values together.

ANSCHE CHESED
251 West 100 Street
New York, NY 10025
Phone: 212/865-0600

Young Professionals, comprised of singles primarily in their 20s and 30s, sponsors a monthly shabbat dinner usually featuring a speaker. The Outings Group hosts activities including hiking, rafting, square dancing, etc. They also have a weekly coed volleyball game on Tuesdays at 7:30 pm attracting singles in their 20s and 30s.

CONGREGATION B'NAI JESHURUN
270 West 88 Street
New York, NY 10024
Phone: 212/787-7600

Singles of all ages participate in activities, including ice skating parties and potluck dinners.

CONGREGATION EMANU-EL
1 East 65 Street
New York, NY 10021
Phone: 212/744-1400, ext. 207

The Emanu-El League is for Reform Jewish singles ages 22-39. Social and religious programs take place monthly. Young Professionals is for singles and couples ages 22-39. The group presents four midweek evening lectures. Reservations are necessary, and there is a buffet, conversation and a Q & A period. Other events include Sabbath Morning Services followed by a Bagel Brunch and A Model Seder.

LINCOLN SQUARE SYNAGOGUE
200 Amsterdam Avenue
New York, NY 10023
Phone: 212/874-6100

The Singles Committee plans events attracting singles primarily in their 30s and 40s. To receive notification of singles activities, you need to send a check for $18. Events include dinners, lecture series, etc.

PARK AVENUE SYNAGOGUE
50 East 87 Street
New York, NY 10128
Phone: 212/369-2600

The Melamed Club for Young Singles holds events for ages 25-40. These include dances, holiday parties, dinners, and workshops.

Audrey Pavey, 34, has attended lectures and says, "The people are friendly, intelligent professionals. The lecture groups are topical discussions of interest and relevant to what's going on in the world today."

SUTTON PLACE SYNAGOGUE
225 East 51 Street
New York, NY 10022
Phone: 212/593-3300

A wide array of events are regularly held for singles, including parties for those in their 20s and 30s and dances for singles age 39+. Events are also held in conjunction with Jewish holidays.

SUFFOLK Y JEWISH SINGLES
74 Hauppauge Road
Commack, NY 11725
Phone: 516/462-9800

Singles ages 21-35 meet Mondays at 8:00 pm at pool parties, volleyball, murder mystery nights, etc. A Rap Group for singles ages 30+ meets Mondays at 8:00 pm. Thursdays at 8:00 pm, singles ages 30+ mingle at various socials, Ping Pong, billiards, board games, volleyball, wine and cheese, etc. Other events include Singles Bridge, Country Western Dance, and museum visits. Check out the annual Conference for Jewish Singles on Long Island usually held in April.

SID JACOBSEN JEWISH COMMUNITY CENTER
300 Forest Drive
East Hills, NY 11548
Phone: 516/484-1545

A variety of singles events for ages 35+ are held, including Sunday Brunches, dances, and Monday Night Bridge.

QUEENS JEWISH SINGLES (QJS)
Flushing Jewish Community Council
41-60 Kissena Boulevard
Flushing, NY 11355
Phone: 718/460-5069

QJS offers workshops, lectures, bowling nights, dances, etc. A bimonthly newsletter lists activities sponsored by various temples throughout Queens and Nassau.

YM-YWHA OF NORTHERN QUEENS
45-35 Kissena Boulevard
Flushing, NY 11355
Phone: 718/461-3198

Events are offered for singles ages 25-39, ages 34-49, and 50+. These include volleyball, tennis parties, dances, bowling, drama workshops, roller skating, and trips to Atlantic City.

TEMPLE BETH-EL OF GREAT NECK
5 Old Mill Road
Great Neck, NY 11023
Phone: 516/484-1545

A variety of events are held for singles, including dances, holiday parties, and discussions.

TEMPLE ISRAEL
108 Old Mill Road
Great Neck, NY 11023
Phone: 516/487-1466 (Young Singles)
and 516/487-1756 (Club "1")

Young Singles hosts Friday night dinners, holiday services, parties, and trips for singles ages 22-39. Club "1," ages 35+, holds Friday night dinners and monthly Sunday breakfasts, in addition to dances, rap groups, etc.

Andrew Nadler, 35, has attended events at Temple Israel and says, "The activities allow you to meet and have a fun time while participating in events and experiences with other people of similar age and background."

SAMUEL FIELD YM-YWHA
58-20 Little Neck Parkway
Little Neck, NY 11362
Phone: 718/225-6750 ext. 243

Every Wednesday at 8:00 pm, there is a lecture/discussion group for singles ages 30-50. Many in their 40s attend.

BETH EL SYNAGOGUE CENTER
Northfield Road at North Avenue
New Rochelle, NY 10804
Phone: 914/235-2700

Beth El Special Times (B.E.S.T.) offers events for Mature Singles 39+ and Singles of All Ages. These include discussions, dances, and shabbat dinners.

MID-ISLAND Y JEWISH COMMUNITY CENTER
45 Manetto Hill Road
Plainview, NY 11803
Phone: 516/822-3535

Mid-Singles Connection, appealing primarily to singles ages 35-55, meets every Thursday for a casual evening of games, dancing, discussion, etc. Approximately 30-45 people attend. Dances are also held for singles ages 30+.

WESTCHESTER JEWISH CONFERENCE
701 Westchester Avenue, Suite 203E
White Plains, NY 10604
Phone: 914/761-5100

The Singles Network is a volunteer-run organization for Jewish singles of Westchester County. They publish a newsletter listing events sponsored by various groups, the YM & YWHA, and temples.

JCC ON THE PALISADES
411 East Clinton Avenue
Tenafly, NJ 07670
Phone: 201/569-7900

Young Singles—ages 21-39
Singles on the Palisades—ages 40+
Palisades Sociables—ages 35-49

All of these groups host a wide array of socializing opportunities including parties, wine tastings, brunches, bowling bashes, sports nights, acting classes, dancing, and discussion groups. Call to receive a copy of their monthly newsletter.

Off the Beaten Track

@ @ @

They say you can't judge a book by its cover, and this is often true of a Mensch. But it has never been said that you can't meet the love of your life while immersed in a book. For those with a literary bent, mingling opportunities abound at bookstores, poetry readings, and possibly even the NY Public Library.

However, if books are not your thing, it may be time to take up a hobby or renew other interests. Consider exploring such options as singing, foreign languages, cars, or astrology, and you may find yourself in good company. NYC dog lovers, too, have a place to convene. Or, if the thought of school brings back fond memories, perhaps take a class or join your alumni organization.

You may be thinking, sure if I only had the time. If this sounds like you, don't discount meeting opportunities during the course of your everyday routine. Even the workplace itself or a professional organization may present romantic opportunities. I have known people to meet and marry through commuting on the Long Island Railroad. Pick a car, sit there routinely, and notice people around you. Under these circumstances, it's fairly easy to strike up a conversation. The truth is you may meet Mr. Right anywhere, anytime!

For Book Worms

BARNES & NOBLE
2289 Broadway (82nd Street)
New York, NY 10027
Phone: 212/362-8835

While browsing for a title, you may find yourself mingling with others and stopping for a bite at The Cafe which is open until midnight on Friday and Saturday.

BORDERS BOOKS & MUSIC
1260 Old Country Road
Westbury, NY 11590
Phone: 516/683-8888

Lectures, poetry nights, live music, and discussion groups are some of the activities offered at these mega-stores. Inquire about special singles nights. Check out the monthly calendar of events available in-store. There are also locations in Bohemia (516/244-7496) and Levittown (516/579-6880).

SINGLE BOOKLOVERS
Box 117
Gradyville, PA 19039
Phone: 215/358-5049

Single Booklovers publishes a monthly letter that provides members with two-line descriptive sketches about each other. If you want to know more about someone, you write to Single Booklovers and are sent a copy of their Personal Profile Sheet. There are 1,400 members of all ages.

Public Shows

If you have a particular interest in boats, cars, or comics, you may want to visit the public shows held at the following locations:

JACOB K. JAVITS CONVENTION CENTER
655 West 34 Street
New York, NY 10001
212/216-2000

There is a Boat Show, New York International Automobile Show, and Art Show.

NASSAU COLISEUM
1255 Hempstead Turnpike
Uniondale, NY 11553
516/794-9303

Check out the Custom Car Show, Empire State Beer-Tasting Festival, Consumer Electronics and Computers, and Long Island Card and Comic Expo.

Specialized Groups

ASTRO DATING CLUB
Manhattan School of Astrology
P.O. Box 20217
New York, NY 10011
Phone: 212/633-9878

When you join, professional astrologers find you compatible mates. You supply them with your date, time, and place of birth and a little about yourself, and you receive an astrological chart. Your profile is checked against other members on file for compatability signs, and you receive information on compatible matches.

THE LANGUAGE CLUB
2211 Broadway, Suite 3A
New York, NY 10024
Phone: 212/787-2110

While not expressly for singles, this Club sponsors gatherings for those with a penchant for foreign language. Approximately 20 people of all ages gather to converse over dinner or brunch at a NYC restaurant on Mondays at 6:00 pm and Sundays at noon.

SINGLES THAT SING
Phone: 201/343-6447

Bill Carr, a former vocal coach, founded this group attracting singles of all ages with all degrees of talent. Gatherings, held a couple of times a month in Hackensack, NJ, are typically attended by a dozen or so people who take the microphone in hand and belt out their favorite tune.

Beth Grout, 30, joined the group because "I've always been attracted to men that sing," she says. "There's a variety of personalities there, and it beats the high pressure, meet market of the bar scene."

Professional Groups

You might attend events of a professional organization in your field. For example, the NY Chapter of the American Marketing Association holds meetings and holiday parties that present networking opportunities, both social and professional. Check publications such as Crain's New York Business for weekly listings.

Miscellaneous

NUYORICAN POETS CAFE
236 East 3 Street
New York, NY 10009
Phone: 212/780-9386

This café holds poetry readings by young emerging poets that attract singles in their mid 20s-mid 30s. The most popular night is Friday at 7:30 pm with about 100 in attendance, but readings are also held on Wednesday at 7:30 pm.

DOG RUN
81st Street, near Columbus Avenue

Part of Margaret Mead Green, a park next to the Museum of Natural History, this is one of five fenced in areas for dogs scattered around the city. Dogs fraternize and run around unleashed, and dog owners mingle and compare notes on canine care. It can be quite a social scene, particularly on weeknights and Sunday afternoons. Come with or without a dog.

Classes

LEARNING ANNEX
116 East 85 Street
New York, NY 10028
Phone: 212/570-6500

Three of the Annex's classes designed expressly for meeting are:
IceBreakers
The Musical Meeting Party for Singles
The New Getting Together Party

NEW YORK UNIVERSITY
SCHOOL OF CONTINUING EDUCATION
100 Washington Square East
New York, NY 10003
Phone: 212/998-7080

Metropolitan Experience for Young Professionals:
This long-running program is designed for active, career-minded professionals. Each week you explore a facet of city life in the classroom through lectures by key personalities and in off-site visits to theaters, restaurants, museums, concerts, etc. There is a social hour after each session. Speakers have included Dr. Ruth Westheimer, former Mayor Ed Koch, and representatives from Sotheby's. The cost is $295 for eight sessions.

92ND STREET Y
1395 Lexington Avenue
New York, NY 10128
Phone: 212/996-1100

The Y offers a Singles Lectures series on Sundays at 7:30 pm featuring broadcasters, actors, authors, etc. A reception with refreshments follows each program. There is also a Saturday Night Singlespeaks at 7:30 pm, where singles discuss issues pertaining to being single in NYC. Social hours with refreshments precede and follow rap groups. The age range is mixed.

From the Mouths of Mensches

⊚ ⊚ ⊚

*I*t's true that no two Mensches are the same, though they share certain inherent traits, as we've identified. Now that you know how to recognize one, how do you snare one and ultimately make your way down the aisle?

In an effort to shed some light on this subject, I've assembled a panel of both single and married men and women who were open enough to share their views and good-natured enough to maintain a sense of humor about it. All were asked to respond to three questions, and below are selected comments that I thought would be of the most interest.

The Panel

MEN

Eric Geltman, 32, Construction Management Entrepreneur, married 1 1/2 years

Alex Harris, 31, Telecommunications Executive, engaged to be married

David Konig, 32, host of HBO's Hardcore TV, married 3 years

David Krinsky, 33, Immigration Inspector, married 3+ years

Peter Reiser, 31, Attorney, single

Alan Rogowsky, 47, Attorney, single

Scott Travers, 32, Rare Coin Broker/Dealmaker, single

WOMEN

Allison Cohen, 41, Marketing Consultant, single

Susan Heit, 36, Telecommunications Senior Project Manager, single

Annette Krasner, 31, Manager Client Services, single

Beth Mason, 33, Marketing Consultant, married 11 years

Susan Stern, 31, Public Relations Consultant, single

Judy Tenzer, 27, Public Relations Executive, single

Cindy Zelson, 35, Attorney, single

First Question: In your eyes, what characterizes a Mensch?

Reiser: "A guy mensch puts the seat down when he's done; and a girl mensch does not get upset when he forgets."

Krinsky: "Somebody who does something you really want to do, but he doesn't. But, he does it so well that everyone around is convinced it was his idea."

Geltman: "Someone who doesn't take you to an early bird special on the first date."

Harris: "A mensch is self confident and unselfish, treating the significant person in his life not as an entitlement, but rather as a bonus."

Stern: "A mensch is a lovable guy who always considers other people's feelings before his own."

Zelson: "Confident, but not cocky. Sincere, genuine, doesn't play games. Listens and asks questions about you."

Tenzer: "He remembers your birthday, calls when you're sick, and doesn't set a stop watch when he's waiting for you to prepare for a date."

Second Question:
What advice would you give to someone seeking to meet a Mensch?

Travers: "You don't often meet a mensch; you get to know someone and find out later. Toss away first impressions; a potential spouse will appear more sexually atttractive, anyway, after building a friendship."

Krinsky: "Don't look for a perfect fit in an off-the-rack world."

Harris: "Recognize your own human weaknesses and work on them. Don't let these weaknesses serve as the basis for your attraction to or attractiveness to another person."

Rogowsky: "Keep trying. Waiting around for that right 'somebody' to come to you will keep you at home. You have to keep up your energy level and look for every opportunity to come into contact with others trying to do the same! Remember—it is the right SOMEbody you want, not the right someBODY!"

Reiser: "When attending an event, women should go in pairs. Large gaggles are intimidating; women alone are slightly suspect. (P.S. It doesn't hurt if you're better looking than your friend.)"

Geltman: "Don't go out with anybody who your grandmother wants to set you up with. But seriously, going out with a group of friends is always a good idea because meeting someone in a group scenario is less pressure, and if you click, you can get to know the person casually before going on a date."

Heit: "Open your eyes and look at your friends...maybe Mr. Right is in front of your nose."

Mason: "Don't search. This person will be your best friend before anything else. If you expect too much, you will be sorely disappointed. No one, not even you, is perfect."

Third Question:
How would you know if you met the Mensch you should marry?

Konig: "You will receive official written notification from the National Mensch Foundation, with valuable coupons."

Reiser: "You're going to be stranded on a desert island and can only bring one thing. If he's the thing you'd bring, he's the mensch to marry."

Cohen: "If you think you'd feel good about waking up next to this person everyday for the rest of your life, you're there. Seriously, if you share things in common, especially your goals and values, if you can trust each other, and if you're in love, those are pretty good signs."

Heit: "When you write his name in ink in your phone book."

Mason: "If you have to ask, then you haven't met the right person. Like Sleepless in Seattle, you know. You enjoy this person's company. You're equals and work together. You like similar things. Each will want to do separate things at time, and you make room for that. Compromise is part of the process, and both sides participate. It can't be one sided."

Krasner: "You have your wisdom teeth pulled, and he brings you chocolate shakes, and loves you even though your face is swollen."

The Light at the End of the Tunnel

How would I answer Question #3?

If you are at ease, content, and confident about the relationship when you're away from your love interest, that's a good sign.

Further Advice—

How you feel when you're not with the person is equally, if not more important, than how you feel on a date. Don't mistake post-date heartburn and stomach flutters for true love. It may just be the calamari in chili sauce you shared at dinner.

Anxiety does not mean excitement, and frustration is not a substitute for passion. You may think you're excited because of what you know, but in reality, it may be because of what you don't know. At the beginning of a relationship you are filled with the anticipation of what could be, but infatuation is not a basis for marriage. After all, that Cloud Nine feeling doesn't last forever, and Cloud Eight is certainly nothing to sneeze at.

A person may be fun for a night on the town, but when it comes to spending a lifetime, you need to look past nocturnal compatibility. Being realistic about what you expect in a relationship does not mean radically compromising your standards. It just means accepting that it is not possible for one person to have all the qualities you seek.

Learn from past mistakes. If you have a tendency to reapeat a pattern, take a hard look at your choices. You are probably dating the wrong kinds of men. Read the signals, and trust your instincts. Have respect for yourself. You deserve to be treated well. In every relationship, vibes are given off, but sometimes we choose not to see. Take the Ray Bans off and pop some Visine.

They always say it happens when you least expect it, and like many, I was as surprised as anyone.

It may sound trite, but if you open your mind, and your heart, anything is possible. Take it from one who knows.

Update: 100+ More Ways to Meet a Mensch

Since bringing the first edition of this book to you in October '94, I have continued to research the ever-evolving singles scene, and I have uncovered over 100 additional social activities/organizations worthy of your attention. It seems there are always new approaches to meeting a mensch in the tri-state area, and that means you should never run out of things to do in your search for a mate.

The key is to take risks, try new things, and pursue interest-oriented activities. If you've been doing the same thing for the last ten years, and it hasn't worked for you, it's time to try something new. Break old patterns, cultivate new interests, and most importantly, be a savvy single and socialize "strategically." What that means is that you need to put yourself where you're going to find the opposite sex in numbers. These opportunities really do abound if you know where to look, and I have done the homework for you. Enjoy!! And, remember, there is no such thing as a "perfect mensch," so go forward with an open mind.

Mix 'n' Mingle

SPARKLE
459 Columbus Avenue, Suite 179
New York, NY 10132
Phone: 800/99-SPARKLE

Socials for Jewish professionals in their 20s and 30s.

UTOPIA
P.O. Box 4444
New York, NY 10185-4444
Phone: 212/459-4321

Socials for Jewish professionals in their 20s and 30s.

STAN & JEFF'S PARTIES
Phone: 718/428-6447

Dance parties at clubs in NYC with live entertainment for upscale singles from late 20s-early 40s. Also hosts a dude ranch weekend.

CAROLYN'S TALK OF THE TOWN SINGLES
42 Remsen Street, Suite 4
Brooklyn, NY 11201
Phone: 718/875-3878

Elegant, candlelit soirees for upbeat professional, business, and creative people at private Manhattan homes. Host makes personal introductions.

EYE-TO-EYE SINGLES
5624 17th Avenue
Brooklyn, NY 11204
Phone: 718/232-4249

Plans varied social activities for Orthodox Jewish singles, ages 28-48, in the tri-state area.

SINGLE ELEGANCE
3280 Sunrise Highway, Suite 367
Wantaugh, NY 11793
Phone: 516/221-8122

A private club on Long Island for professional singles, 30-55.
Applicants are interviewed for membership. Activities include
lectures, museum tours, physical fitness nights, picnics, cruises,
and day trips.

TWENTIES & THIRTIES
8 Juliet Lane
Northport, NY 11768
Phone: 516/261-6215

This singles group on the North Shore of Long Island hosts intimate events which include dining, dancing, and fitness outings.

SENSATIONS
55 Old Turnpike Rd., Suite 301
Nanuet, NY 10954
Phone: 914/645-1654

Parties at clubs in NYC for upscale professionals in their 30s
and 40s.

P.J. SINGLES
P.O. Box 293
Springfield, NJ 07081-0293
Phone: 201/258-0022

Dances for professional Jewish singles, 21-45, throughout
New Jersey.

TASTEBUDS, INC.
434 Ridgedale Avenue, Suite 11-149
East Hanover, NJ 07936
Phone: 201/515-8825

A private club that sponsors dinner socials, cocktail parties, scavenger hunts, hikes, theatre outings, wine & beer tastings, and sports
activities. Attracts singles in their 20s - 40s; events are throughout
New Jersey.

Up, Up and Away

BLUE MOUNTAIN LODGE
1905 Old Kings Highway
P.O. Box 63
Saugerties, NY 12477
Phone: 914/246-8711

This Catskill Mountains resort hosts activity-filled singles weekends in a rustic country environment for a 40-something crowd.

DYNAMO DAVE'S DISCOVERY TOURS, INC.
85-30 121 Street
Kew Gardens, NY 11415
Phone: 718/847-4698 or 800/646-9260

Bicycle tours in NY, Florida, New England, and other areas attract an intimate group of singles and others ages 30-50. Kosher food is available.

VACATION CONNECTION
18711 Tiffeni Drive, Suite 17
Twain Harte, CA 95383
Phone: 209/586-9538

This company puts singles in touch with other vacationing singles and locals at popular vacation areas. Once you plan a trip, you are given the names of singles with similar interests who will be at your destination. You can contact them before and during your trip.

SUMMER SHARES - BELMAR, NEW JERSEY
Schlossbach Realty
Phone: 908/681-4277

The shore town of Belmar is located about an hour from Manhattan, and features many popular bars and restaurants. Great for the 20-something crowd.

For the Sports-Minded

BOWLMOR LANES
110 University Place
New York, NY 10003
Phone: 212/255-8188

From midnight bowls to weekend bowls, this is a happening spot for those looking to score (a strike . . . that is).

CHELSEA PIERS
23rd Street and the Hudson
New York, NY 10011
Phone: 212/336-6000

This amazing sports facility offers everything from golf to rock climbing to batting cages. Without a doubt, the ultimate meeting spot for the athletically-inclined.

THE CITY CLIMBERS CLUB
Parks & Recreation Building
59th Street between 10th and 11th Avenues
New York, NY 10019
Phone: 212/974-2250

This indoor climbing club features a great climbing wall and offers lessons.

CLAREMONT RIDING ACADEMY
175 West 89 Street
New York, NY 10024
Phone: 212/724-5100

If horseback riding is for you, check out this female-dominated riding academy where you ride English style in Central Park.

OUTDOOR BOUND INC.
18 Stuyvesant Oval, Suite 1A
New York, NY 10009
Phone: 212/505-1020

Over 100 outings and weekend trips year-round feature outdoor
recreation and wilderness activities from hiking, canoeing, rafting,
and kayaking to skiing.

LONG ISLAND SINGLE SAILORS ASSOCIATION, INC.
P.O. Box 370
Huntington, NY 11743
Phone: 516/547-1010

Sponsors nautical events, plus movie and theatre nights, dances
and parties, hikes, bike rides, ski weekends, and canoe trips.
Members must be at least 30.

Parties for a Purpose

JEWISH BOARD OF FAMILY & CHILDREN'S SERVICES (JBFCS)
120 West 57 Street
New York, NY 10019
Phone: 212/582-9100

The JBFCS is the nation's premiere voluntary mental health and
social service agency. The Alliance hosts fundraising social and
educational events for singles from 25-45, and has a matchmaking
service called LINKS.

THE PARKS COUNCIL ASSOCIATES
457 Madison Avenue
New York, NY 10022
Phone: 212/838-9410, Ext. 222

This is the 40 and under arm of the Parks Council, dedicated
to keeping NY green through fundraising events that educate
concerned New Yorkers.

SOCIETY OF MEMORIAL SLOAN-KETTERING
CANCER CENTER
1233 York Avenue
New York, NY 10021
Phone: 212/639-7972

The Associates Committee plans fundraisers for singles in their 20s and 30s.

WOMEN'S AMERICAN ORT
315 Park Avenue South
New York, NY 10010
Phone: 212/505-7700 ext. 244

This Jewish non-profit organization works to improve public education, promote literacy, combat anti-Semitism, support women's rights and fund technical and vocational schools throughout the world. The NYC Chapter sponsors events for singles ages 25-45, including dances and lectures.

YOUTH RENEWAL FUND
165 East 65 Street
New York, NY 10022
Phone: 212/207-3195

This non-profit organization is dedicated to providing supplemental education to under-privileged Jewish, Israeli youth. Events attracting singles in their 20s and 30s include dinner dances, theater outings, and basketball tournaments.

MARCH OF DIMES BIRTH DEFECTS FOUNDATION
155 Foundation Plaza
East Hartford, CT 06108-3211
Phone: 203/290-5440

The Connecticut March of Dimes, a non-profit organization dedicated to preventing birth defects, has been sponsoring its annual Bid for Bachelors since 1986. Check for their other social events and programs.

Cultural Encounters

THE BALLROOM REVIEW
60 Gramercy Park North
New York, NY 10010
Phone: 212/673-3442

This newsletter/guide features hot spots for dancing in the tri-state area, dance weekends, and articles of interest to the dance enthusiast. It's published eight times a year.

THE CENTER CIRCLE
Lincoln Center Productions
Phone: 212/875-5444

Members (socially conscious professional New Yorkers under 40) have access to events including concerts, rehearsals and private receptions with various artists.

LINCOLN CENTER OFF STAGE
Lincoln Center Productions
Phone: 212/875-5440

Hosts meet-the-artist conversations followed by wine and cheese receptions.

LUSH LIFE FOR SINGLE JAZZ LOVERS
P.O. Box 239
New Rochelle, NY 10804
Phone: 212/229-7888

Singles in their late 30s-50 attend parties and listen to jazz at NYC's legendary jazz clubs and enjoy a free buffet.

MIDSUMMER NIGHT SWING
Lincoln Center Productions
70 Lincoln Center Plaza
New York, NY 10023-6583
Phone: 212/875-5102

Every June and July, Midsummer Night Swing features 20 nights of mambo, swing, tango, and more, to popular dance bands in the specially created outdoor dance club on Lincoln Center's Fountain Plaza.

SOLO ARTS GROUP, INC.
36 West 17 Street
New York, NY 10011
Phone: 212/463-8732

Check the newspapers for special singles mixer nights at this Off-Off-Broadway theater. Funny shows have included "Jumping Off the Fridge" with Ellen Hulkower.

SOLOMON R. GUGGENHEIM MUSEUM
1071 Fifth Avenue
New York, NY 10128
Phone: 212/423-3534

The Guggenheim Circle is a special leadership group for young professionals from 21 - 40 with an interest in modern and contemporary art. There are monthly social and education programs.

MUSIC AND ART LOVERS CLUB FOR SINGLES
1401 Ocean Avenue
Brooklyn, NY 11230
Phone: 718/252-5683

This quarterly newsletter features brief bios of members to contact.

NEW COMMUNITY CINEMA
423 Park Avenue
Huntington, NY 11743
Phone: 516/423-7653

Holds periodic singles nights with mingling after films.

SINGLE LOVERS OF THE ARTS
300 Main Street, Suite 258
Huntington, NY 11743
Phone: 516/673-1466

Arts-loving members, mostly from NYC and Long Island, receive a monthly newsletter featuring descriptions of other members to contact.

ANTIQUE LOVERS
P.O. Box 363
Devon, PA 19333
Phone: 610/341-1950

Offers personal ads in their newsletter, plans trips, socials and other exciting events for singles interested in antiques and collectibles.

THE MOVIE CLUB
P.O. Box 4092
River Edge, NJ 07661
Phone: 201/342-8609

Holds movie outings in NY and NJ, followed by dinner and discussion.

Computer Compatibility

CUPID'S NETWORK
URL: http://www.cupidnet.com

This is the world's largest network of romantic eligibles on the Internet. The site links to nationwide singles services, publications, matchmakers, travel groups, personal ad services, and has a calendar of singles events.

Personals/Reading Material

METRO SPORTS MAGAZINE
27 West 24 Street, Suite 10B
New York, NY 10010
Phone: 212/627-7040

This complimentary magazine features organizations, outings, articles and personal ads for the sports enthusiast.

Hfow to Meet a Mensch in New York

NEW YORK OBSERVER
"Personal Dialogue"
P.O. Box 8208
New York, NY 10150
Phone: 212/688-6935

This weekly newspaper read largely by execs in the publishing
and advertising arenas is a good option for those seeking a
creative-type.

NEW YORK PRESS
295 Lafayette Street
New York, NY 10012-2722
Phone: 212/941-1130

This free weekly newspaper, readily available on the streets
of NYC, has an extensive personal ad section and sponsors socials
for singles.

NEW YORK PURSUITS
P.O. Box 2004
New York, NY 10021
Phone: 212/439-9055

Taking courses is a great way to meet people, and this paperback
book lists adult education courses at over 100 schools in the NY
metropolitan area.

THE RELATIONSHIP LINE
1556 Third Avenue, #402
New York, NY 10128
Phone: 212/987-7000

An upscale, voice-mail, personal ad service where you can listen to
thousands of ads, respond and even place your own. They also host
monthly dance parties at clubs in NYC. For ages 25-49.

SINGLES NEWS & VIEWS
P.O. Box 1304
New York, NY 10028
Phone: 516/520-9418

This monthly newspaper lists singles events in the tri-state area.

♥ 114 ♥

THE SOLO REPORT
c/o E.T. White
22 E. 89 Street, #2D
New York, NY 10128
Phone: 212/860-2178

This newsletter, for professional singles from 30-55, features witty essays and articles celebrating singlehood.

SPORTS CITY
306 West 92 Street
New York, NY 10025
Phone: 212/580-7400

This free magazine features lists of sporting activities, plus articles and personals for the athletically-inclined.

TIME OUT NEW YORK
627 Broadway, 7th Floor
New York, NY 10012
Phone: 212/539-4430

This weekly magazine is a highly comprehensive guide to all the city has to offer. It includes a personal ad section.

BROOKLYN BRIDGE
388 Atlantic Avenue
Brooklyn, NY 11217
Phone: 718/596-7400 ext. 103

This glossy monthly magazine includes personal ads.

SINGLE LIVING MAGAZINE
P.O. Box 695
Yonkers, NY 10704
Phone: 914/376-5444

This national magazine covers relationships, leisure, art, music, cooking and parenting with a singles slant. It also sponsors activities for singles.

THE BACHELORETTE BOOK
THE BACHELOR BOOK
8222 Wiles Rd., Ste. 111
Coral Springs, FL 33067-1937
Phone: 800/766-7557

Two magazines—for single women and gentlemen—featuring articles and profiles/photos of singles with contact information.

NEW YORK'S DIVORCE MAGAZINE
3 Dault Road
Scarborough, ON MIN 1E6
Phone: 416/691-8441

This magazine features articles of broad interest to divorced singles.

The Personal Approach: Matchmakers and Dating Services

BLUMBERG INTRODUCTIONS
230 Park Avenue, Suite 1000
New York, NY 10169
Phone: 212/808-3054

For non-Orthodox Jewish professionals in their 20s-40s. In-depth consultations are conducted, and matches are made.

PROVIDENCE MATCHMAKING SERVICES, INC.
575 Madison Avenue, Suite 1006
New York, NY 10022
Phone: 212/605-0282

Providence makes matches based primarily on family background and psychological makeup of both you and the partner you seek.

SOLUTION FOR SINGLES
2175 Lemoine Avenue, Suite 500
Fort Lee, NJ 07024
Phone: 201/944-6171

A personalized introduction service for the "busy professional and business executive." See photos of members and discuss profiles of those you may like to meet.

TOGETHER
161 Worcester Road
Framingham, MA 01701
Phone: 800/717-1007

The world's largest personal introduction network with over 175 offices.

NOTE: Keep in mind the phone number for the International Society of Introduction Services, a trade group for the dating industry. When in doubt, give them a call at 818/222-1367 or 707/765-1526.

Wining and Dining

PETER KUMP'S SCHOOL OF CULINARY ARTS
50 West 23 Street
New York, NY 10010
Phone: 212/242-2882
307 East 92 Street
New York, NY 10028
Phone: 212/410-4601

Both locations offer a variety of cooking classes for singles, attracting an intimate group predominantly ages 30-45.

WINDOWS ON THE WORLD WINE SCHOOL
1 World Trade Center, 106th Fl.
New York, NY 10048
Phone: 914/255-1456

Many of the students in this eight-week course are bankers, Wall Streeters, and food professionals. Attracts 80-100 students.

NEW YORK WINE TASTING SCHOOL
32 Bergen Street
Brooklyn, NY 11201
Phone: 718/852-4839

Three classes are offered per year, attracting an intimate crowd of both marrieds and singles.

DINNER INTRODUCTIONS
44 Kyle Court
Staten Island, NY 10312
Phone: 718/227-2335

Plans cocktail parties and group dinners for compatible singles.

MIXERS HOSTED BY LIQUOR COMPANIES
Dewars—Phone: 800-8DEWARS
Tanqueray—Phone: 800-9JENKINS

These are just two of the liquor companies that sponsor social events at local bars where the drinks flow as freely as the conversation.

Meeting on Common Ground

THE JEWISH COMMUNITY CENTER
ON THE UPPER WEST SIDE
15 West 65 Street, 8th Floor
New York, NY 10023
Phone: 212/580-0099

The Associates and Young Associates are singles and couples in their 20s and 30s who participate in social, educational, volunteer, and recreational events.

PARENTS OF ADULT JEWISH SINGLES (PAJES)
103 Beethoven Avenue
Waban, MA 02168
Phone: 617/332-4482

PAJES publishes a National Registry of Adult Jewish Singles, featuring profiles of members, arranged geographically. Members are mostly professionals from 20-67. Parents may call up, in addition to singles themselves, but information is mailed discreetly only to the single.

UAHC NEW JERSEY/WEST HUDSON VALLEY COUNCIL
1 Kalisa Way
Paramus, NJ 07652
Phone: 201/599-0080

This non-profit organization publishes the "Reform Jewish Singles Directory," serving singles ages 21 and older throughout New Jersey and several counties in New York. Members pay a nominal fee to have their profile featured in a directory made available at a dozen temples.

JEWISH INTRODUCTION NETWORK (JIN)
5 Old Mill Road
Great Neck, NY 11023
Phone: 516/487-0900

Similar to the above; synagogues on Long Island currently participate.

FIFTH AVENUE SYNAGOGUE
5 East 62 Street
New York, NY 10021
Phone: 212/838-2122

The Young Leadership group sponsors holiday celebrations and other activities attracting marrieds and singles from 20-40s.

THE SUFFOLK Y JCC
74 Hauppauge Road
Commack, NY 11725
Phone: 516/462-9800

Holds a wide variety of activities for Jewish singles of all ages, including divorced, parents, widows and widowers.

CATHOLIC SINGLES MATCHING CLUB
P.O. Box 6428
Jersey City, NJ 07306
Phone: 201/451-1012 or212/366-0446

Has chapters throughout New York, New Jersey, and Connecticut for member singles from 20-69. (Note: they also have a College Graduates Matching Club which is for singles of mixed Christian religions.)

CATHOLIC EXECUTIVES ORGANIZATION (CEO)
P.O. Box 2556, Times Square Post Office
New York, NY 10108
Phone: 212/627-0010

CEO is a service that matches corporate presidents, entrepreneurs, executives, doctors, lawyers, academics, and achievers in other professions with their equally successful counterparts.

CATHOLIC SINGLES ASSOCIATION
P.O. Box 406
Yonkers, NY 10704
Phone: 914/428-9042

This organization sponsors dances at hotels, picnics, boat rides, and ski trips for singles from 25-49, with 500 members in the metropolitan area.

LONG ISLAND CATHOLIC SINGLES CLUB
P.O. Box 476
Lindenhurst, NY 11757
Phone: 516/736-2330

Offers social activities on Long Island for singles from 25-45.

DIVORCED AND SEPARATED CATHOLICS (DSC)
Nassau County No. 1 P.O. Box 883
Hicksville, NY 11802-0883
Phone: 516/931-6963

DSC is a non-profit, non-sectarian organization devoted to the welfare and interest of single persons and their families. The monthly newsletter features discussion groups, and lists house parties, weekend trips, plus activities for the young singles group, widows and widowers group, and retirees.

SINGLE CHRISTIAN NETWORK
Box 3282
Olathe, KS 66063
Phone: 913/829-5765

Members provide personal information to the network, then each month receive profiles of other singles who match the descriptions of people they're seeking.

THE CATHOLIC ALUMNI CLUB
83 Christopher Street
New York, NY 10014
Phone: 212/243-0901

This club for single, Catholic college grads sponsors activities including theatre, opera and movie outings, dinner socials, workshops, and parties.

IRISH AMERICAN SINGLES ASSOCIATION
P.O. Box 34
Lynbrook, NY 11563
Phone: 516/825-8899

Sponsors dinner outings and day trips.

Looking for Kindred Spirits

WELL-ROUNDED CLUB
P.O. Box 3504
Cranston, RI 02910
Phone: 401/496-8650

Catering to plus-size singles, this club runs dance parties and dinners in CT. Personal ads are also featured in the newsletter.

LARGE ENCOUNTERS
P.O. Box 364
Island Park, NY 11558-0364
Phone: 516/763-6100 or 718/322-0700

Dance parties in NY, NJ, and CT for "big beautiful ladies and the men who adore them." Personal ads are in the newsletter.

GODDESSES
P.O. Box 1008, J.A.F. Station
New York, NY 10116
Phone: 718/386-1076

Parties for "big, beautiful women and their admirers" in NYC and CT.

PARENTS WITHOUT PARTNERS
Phone: 516/798-3944

Socials for single parents are held at various Long Island venues.

SINGLE PARENT ACTION NETWORK
North Shore Child and Family Guidance Center
480 Old County Road
Roslyn Heights, NY 11577
Phone: 516/997-2926

This support group is devoted to helping singles and their children during the transition that follows a marital separation or divorce.

PARENT CONNECTION
JCC on the Hudson
371 S. Broadway
Tarrytown, NY 10591
Phone: 914/366-7898

Single parents, with children through age 10, socialize over dinner and other events.

YOUNG SINGLE PARENT GROUP
Sid Jacobson Jewish Community Center
300 Forest Drive
East Hills, NY 11548
Phone: 516/484-1545

This singles group for parents with children under age 18 hosts socials, sports activities, and discussion groups.

JEWISH SINGLES PARENTS NETWORK
Temple Beth Shalom
193 East Mt. Pleasant Avenue
Livingston, NJ 07902
Phone: 908/906-6383

Sponsors parent/child activities for parents in their mid 20s-40s.

LENOX HILL NEIGHBORHOOD ASSOCIATION
331 E. 70 Street
New York, NY 10021
Phone: 212/744-5022

Hosts a Single Parent Support Group.

THE TALL CLUB OF NEW YORK CITY
244 Madison Avenue, Suite 281
New York, NY 10016
Phone: 212/332-0067

This non-profit social organization, with chapters nationwide and in Europe, sponsors social, cultural, athletic events, and weekend trips. Women must be at least 5'10", and men should be 6'2" or more. Members receive a monthly calendar of events and a newsletter called "Tall Metropolis."

TRI-COUNTY TALLS
P.O. Box 662
Shelton, CT 06484
Phone: 914/422-LONG

With the same height requirements as The Tall Club, this non-profit organization serves singles in suburban NY and CT. Get-togethers include house parties, dinner dances, and sports outings.

PHYSICALLY DISABLED SINGLES
Greater Five Towns YM & YWHA
207 Grove Avenue, P.O. Box 336
Cedarhurst, NY 11516
Phone: 516/569-6733

Varied activities include movie outings, talent shows, and dinner socials.

BLACK SINGLES RESOURCES
P.O. Box 123
Mt. Vernon, NY 10551
Phone: 914/667-5221

This group's 200 members gather to socialize and explore issues about being single. Activities in the tri-state area include discussion workshops, trips, dances, and game nights. Attracts ages 30-50.

CHINA INSTITUTE
125 E. 65 Street
New York, NY 10021
Phone: 212/744-8181

The Institute holds mixers, gallery opening and other special programs and classes for the Asian-American community. They also have a young professionals club.

For the Young at Heart

GEORGE BERNARD'S PRIVATE PARTIES
345 East 73 Street, #6J
New York, NY 10021
Phone: 212/249-3636

Socials at various locations throughout NYC, often featuring complimentary hors d'oeuvres and munchies. (Bernard also has a group for ages 28-39.)

L.E.A.F. INTERNATIONALE LTD.
4 Park Avenue, Suite 12B
New York, NY 10016
Phone: 212/779-0642

L.E.A.F. (Life Exists After Forty) activities include dances, comedy nights, trips, and other events for members.

UNITED SYNAGOGUE OF CONSERVATIVE JUDAISM
155 Fifth Avenue
New York, NY 10010
Phone: 212/533-7800

There are two singles groups here. Mature Singles offers activities for those 48 and older. Connections sponsors events for singles from 22-38.

ES NORTH SHORE SINGLES EVENTS
88 Chestnut Lane
Woodbury, NY 11797
Phone: 516/335-7071

Hosts dance parties on Long Island attracting professionals ages 30-50.

SINGLE PEOPLE OF TODAY
220 Audley Court
Copaigue, NY 11726
Phone: 718/224-5098 or 516/957-1680

This group hosts a variety of events on Long Island including dances, house parties, picnics, boat rides, and trips for those mid-40s-60.

SINGLES CONNECTION OF WESTCHESTER
Phone: 718/796-1227; Evenings 914/965-3837

This group introduces singles in their 30s-50s at restaurant dinners in the tri-state area, at museum visits, house parties, and day trips. There is also a discussion support group that meets weekly in Scarsdale.

OCEANSIDE JEWISH CENTER
2860 Brower Avenue
Oceanside, NY 11572
Phone: 516/764-6067

The center's Mature Singles group holds monthly meetings and discussion groups for singles over 50.

FREE SONS OF ISRAEL
c/o Burt Feldman
370 West Broadway, 4J
Long Beach, NY 11561
Phone: 516/897-5214

Chai Lodge Singles attracts those 40 and up, for lectures, dances, theatre parties, barbecues, sports outings, day and weekend trips.

RONALD MCDONALD HOUSE
c/o Herb Stone
P.O. Box 24
Jericho, NY 11753
Phone: 516/433-0859

The Singles Clubhouse of this non-profit organization that raises money for Ronald McDonald House hosts socials on Long Island for those 40-60s. You can also participate in their brunches, pool parties, and auctions.

TENNIS SOCIALS
c/o Herb Stone
(see address above)

In Jericho, join 50-70 single tennis players (some even playing doubles) on weekends year-round, weather permitting, to play a few games followed by a casual lunch. No charge for the tennis. Players are 40s-60s.

GOLDEN COMPANIONS (GC)
Box 5249
Reno, NV 89513
Phone: 702/324-2227

A travel companion network, newsletter, and telephone voice-mail service for those 45 and up. GC plans get-togethers and tours, and you can contact members Listed in the Membership Directory.

Miscellaneous

BEVERLY BRIDGE CLUB
130 East 57 Street
New York, NY 10022
Phone: 212/486-9477

Lessons, tournaments, parties, workshops in this popular hangout for bridge afficionados and wannabes.

CONSCIOUS SINGLES CONNECTION (CSC)
243 West End Avenue, Suite 1504
New York, NY 10023-3672
Phone: 212/873-7187

CSC leads you to people interested in personal growth, spiritual practices, holistic health, the arts, science, and the environment. They publish a personal ads newsletter, and sponsor events including dances and workshops.

BINGO PLAYING
Tortilla Flats
767 Washington Street
New York, NY 10014
Phone: 212/243-1053

This is a hot spot for bingo enthusiasts, attracting 20 and 30-somethings who get together to compete and mingle on designated nights.

DRIP
489 Amsterdam Avenue
New York, NY 10024
Phone: 212/875-1032

This Upper West Side coffee bar plays host to "The Lovelife Board." Attracting many 20-something singles, the "Lovelife" bulletin board/looseleaf binder features profiles of hundreds of java-loving eligibles who choose candidates of interest and later rendezvous at Drip for a date arranged by the staff.

FIRST NIGHT NEW YORK
Grand Central Partnership
6 East 43 Street, Suite 2100
New York, NY 10017
Phone: 212/818-1777

Something to do on New Year's Eve! First Night features citywide activities that draw huge international crowds of all ages.

NEW YORK NEW MEDIA ASSOCIATION
55 Broad Street, 11 Floor
New York, NY 10004
Phone: 212/459-4649

The mission of this non-profit organization is to gather together the new media industry in NY. It hosts a free monthly "CyberSuds" networking event.

DOG LOVERS DATING NETWORK
124-28 Queens Boulevard #594
Kew Gardens, NY 11415-1501

You need to write to this group for an application to join.

MENSCH FINDERS
58 Grace Avenue, Suite 2J
Great Neck, NY 11021
Phone: 516/773-0911

If you think you've done it all and need a little coaching on your
social life, make a private appointment with Robin Gorman
Newman. A "personal trainer for your love life," she will make specific recommendations as to where you should go and what you
should do to meet Mr. or Ms. Right.

SINGLES SEMINAR SERIES
Expo Events
1019 Atlantic Avenue
Baldwin, NY 11510
Phone: 516/223-8074

Featuring educational seminars and a showcase of exhibitors with
products and services for singles, they hold expos at various hotels
on Long Island.

ACADEMIC COMPANIONS (AC)
P.O. Box 346
Clinton, NY 13323
Phone: 315/853-5192

AC, a service for bright, interesting singles, publishes a quarterly
periodical featuring personal ads of members.

SCIENCE CONNECTION, INC.
P.O. Box 188
Youngstown, NY 14174-0188
Phone: 800/667-5179

This is a network through which singles interested in nature or science can meet. Members are from all across the U.S. and Canada,
with some from overseas. A monthly newsletter profiles members
to contact.

Mensch-Meeting Coupons

Mensch-Meeting Coupon

It's Just Lunch

Save 10% (up to $50 off) OR get one free date when you join It's Just Lunch. See page 72.

Terms and Conditions: This offer applies only when you join for a minimum of six months.

Mensch-Meeting Coupon

Richnik's

Save $100 on an all-inclusive vacation booked through Richnik's. See page 15.

Terms and Conditions: This coupon must be used on specific all-inclusive vacations.

Mensch-Meeting Coupon

The Roundabout Theatre

Save 20% on a Dewar's Singles Play Series subscription. See page 46.

Terms and Conditions: Mention Code C1 when ordering. Subject to availability.

How to Meet a Mensch in New York

ENJOY.

To redeem your coupon for It's Just Lunch, please call 212/644-0022. And have a great time!

How to Meet a Mensch in New York

ENJOY.

To redeem your coupon at Richnik's Ltd., please call 212/807-0500. And have a great time!

How to Meet a Mensch in New York

ENJOY.

To redeem your coupon at The Roundabout Theatre, please call 212/719-1300. And have a great time!

How to Meet a Mensch in New York

ENJOY.

To redeem your coupon at Echo, please call 212/292-0200.
And have a great time!

How to Meet a Mensch in New York

ENJOY.

To redeem your coupon at The Learning Annex,
please call 212/570-6500. And have a great time!

How to Meet a Mensch in New York

ENJOY.

To redeem your coupon at The Relationshiop Line
please call 212/987-6569. And have a great time!

How to Meet a Mensch in New York

ENJOY.

To redeem your coupon at New York Press, please
call 212/941-1130. And have a great time!

How to Meet a Mensch in New York

ENJOY.

To redeem your coupon at Single Booklovers, please
call 610/358-5049. And have a great time!

How to Meet a Mensch in New York

ENJOY.

To redeem your coupon at Mensch Finders, please
call 516/773-0911. And have a great time!

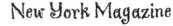

How to Meet a Mensch in New York

ENJOY.

To redeem your coupon at New York Magazine, please
call 212/779-7500. Or fax to 212/779-2449.
And have a great time!

How to Meet a Mensch in New York

ENJOY.

To redeem your coupon at Peter Kump's School of Culinary Arts,
please call 212410-4601. And have a great time!

How to Meet a Mensch in New York

ENJOY.

To redeem your coupon at L.E.A.F. Internationale Ltd.,
please call 212/779-0642. And have a great time!

Mensch-Meeting Coupon

Outdoor Singles

Save $6.00 on an outdoor singles day trip. See page 26.

Terms and Conditions: For new members; may be used one time only. Discount applies to specific trips; call for details.

Mensch-Meeting Coupon

Conscious Singles Connection

Save 10% on the price of a six-month membership. See page 127.

Terms and Conditions: New members only.

Mensch-Meeting Coupon

Time Out New York

Free Personals Ad to run for one week, plus one week of free voicemail service. See page 115.

Terms and Conditions: For more information call 212-539-4430. Offer expires 12/31/97. Limit one per customer.

How to Meet a Mensch in New York

ENJOY.

To redeem your coupon at Outdoor Singles,
please call 718/353-5506. And have a great time!

How to Meet a Mensch in New York

ENJOY.

To redeem your coupon for Conscious Singles Connection,
please call 212/873-7187. And have a great time!

How to Meet a Mensch in New York

ENJOY.

To redeem your coupon at Time Out New York Personals,
send this coupon (along with copy for your four-line Personals
ad) to Tony Monteloene, *Time Out New York* Personals, 627
Broadway, 7th Floor, NY NY 10012. And have a great time!

Mensch-Meeting Coupon

Club Getaway

Save 10% on a weekend vacation package. See page 21.

Terms and Conditions: Discount is applied to the total rate of the package.

Mensch-Meeting Coupon

Tastebuds

Save 30% on a club membership. See page 106.

Terms and Conditions:

Mensch-Meeting Coupon

Second Stage Theatre

Save 20% on a 2, 3 or 4 play singles subscription. See page 47.

Terms and Conditions: For 1996-1997 season only.

How to Meet a Mensch in New York

ENJOY.

To redeem your coupon at Club Getaway, please call 800/6 GETAWAY. And have a great time!

How to Meet a Mensch in New York

ENJOY.

To redeem your coupon at Tastebuds, please call201/515-8825. And have a great time!

How to Meet a Mensch in New York

ENJOY.

To redeem your coupon at Second Stage Theatre, please call 212/787-8302. And have a great time!

Mensch-Meeting Coupon

Single Faces

Free membership, free quarterly newsletter and $2 discount on any event. See page 12.

Mensch-Meeting Coupon

Links

Save $25 on your first 6-month contract for introductions. See page 109.

Terms and Conditions: Good for the first 6-month contract only. LINKS is under the auspices of Jewish Family and Children's Services.

Mensch-Meeting Coupon

New Jersey YM-YWHA Camps

Save 10% on a weekend package. See page 22.

Terms and Conditions: Memorial Day or Labor Day weekend trips only. May be used only once.

How to Meet a Mensch in New York

ENJOY.

To redeem your coupon at Single Faces, please present it at any event; call 908/462-2106 for details and schedule. And have a great time!

How to Meet a Mensch in New York

ENJOY.

To redeem your coupon at LINKS, please call 212/979-1840. And have a great time!

How to Meet a Mensch in New York

ENJOY.

To redeem your coupon at New Jersey YM-YWHA Camps, please call 201/575-3333. And have a great time!

❀ ❀ ❀

In your quest for the ultimate Mensch, let the following acronym be a guide:

M   Keep an open MIND

E   Be ENTHUSIASTIC

N   Act NATURAL

S   SMILE

C   Make CONVERSATION

H   Maintain a sense of HUMOR

❀ ❀ ❀

Reviews of First Edition

"This guide to places and ways to meet "a decent, responsible person even your mother would love" manages to imbue the New York single scene with refreshing optimism. In addition to its anything-is-possible tone, the strength of the book is its comprehensive lists of where singles can meet."
New York Newsday

"If you can't find a mensch among this cornucopia of choices, you're just not looking."
Queens Chronicle

"The guide book blends witty prose with more than 300 lists of off-beat and original places, activities and adventures through which people may just meet their prospective mensches."
The Fresh Meadow Times (Queens, NY)

"Newman lists sources, gives ideas, and lists suggestions on how to find that special someone. From sports to parties, personals to computer dating, the meet market is put into practical perspective."
Brooklyn Woman

"Armed with Gorman Newman's book, you can help others find a good hiking trail, distinguish a cabernet from a sauvignon, and maybe, if you're lucky, reel in a catch to make mommy proud."
The Star Ledger (New Jersey)

"In (this) upbeat and comprehensive guide to Mensch-hunting, Robin advises to give fate a nudge by putting yourself in the right place at the right time."
Jewish Press

"I'm sending my copy to my daughter at college who's simultaneously working on her B.A. in Journalism and her Mrs. in life...this book offers a wealth of pertinent and practical information.
Singles Almanac

"Robin's book has sold by the shedload since it was published. And this slim collection of singles listing is fast spawning a one-woman Mensch industry."
New Woman (London)

Mensch-Meeting Notes

About the Author

Since publishing *How to Meet a Mensch in New York* in October '94, Robin Gorman Newman has become a popular figure on the singles scene. She has lectured extensively as a relationship expert and appeared on television and radio throughout the country. Her articles have been published in *New York Magazine* and the *Daily News*.

Robin is a public relations executive and the founder of Mensch Finders. She is the creative force behind Meet a Mate Week, held annually in June.

She welcomes your comments and particularly wants to hear your stories about finding a mensch. Tell her how you met your mate, especially if it is through one of her suggestions. Write to her c/o City & Company, 22 West 23rd Street, New York, NY 10010.

OTHER TITLES AVAILABLE FROM CITY & COMPANY

Title	Retail
How To Find an Apartment in New York	$12.95
New York Book of Beauty (cloth)	$16.00
New York Cat Owner's Guide	$9.95
New York Book of Coffee & Cake (cloth)	$16.00
Cool Parents Guide to All of New York	$12.95
New York Book of Dance	$14.00
New York Dog Owner's Guide	$9.95
Good & Cheap Ethnic Eats	$9.95
Good & Cheap Vegetarian Dining	$9.95
Jones Guide to Fitness & Health	$9.95
Ken Druse's New York City Gardener	$15.00
How To Make New York a Better Place to Live	$9.95
Marden's Manhattan Booksellers	$15.00
How To Meet A Mensch in New York 2nd Edition	$12.95
New York Book of Music	$15.00
New York Book of Tea (cloth)	$15.00
New York Chocolate Lover's Guide (cloth)	$16.00
New York's 50 Best Nightspots	$9.95
New York's 50 Best Places to Find Peace & Quiet	$9.95
New York's 50 Best Secret Architectural Treasures	$9.95
Psychic New York	$13.00
Shop NY: Downtownstyle	$15.95
Shop NY: Jewelry	$15.95
A Year In New York (cloth)	$20.00

You can find all these books at your local bookstore, or write to:

City & Company 22 West 23rd St New York, NY 10010,
212-366-1988